S0-AYZ-836

CO-028 S

A COMPLETE INTRODUCTION TO
PARROTS

The Red-capped Parrot (Purpureicephalus spurius).

A COMPLETE INTRODUCTION TO

PARROTS

COMPLETELY ILLUSTRATED IN FULL COLOR

A pair of playful Macaws.

Photographs: G. Allen, 41. Toni Angermayer, 68. Glen S. Axelrod, 16, 64. Dr. Herbert R. Axelrod, 5, 17, 22, 29, 31, 33, 34, 52, 63, 77, 105, 116. Cliff Bickford, 87. Courtesy of Bird Depot, Inc., 12, 13. S. Bischoff, 43, 58. T. Brosset, 72. Dr. E.W. Burr, 32. Tom Caravaglia, 79, 86, 126–127. Chelman & Petrulla, 26. John Daniel, 54. K. Donneley, 44. Michael Gilroy, 37. Michael W. Gos, 24. J. Gould, 93. Ray Hanson, 27. Fred Harris, 21, 38, 39, 48, 81. Courtesy of Dr. F.W. Huchzermeyer, 28. P. Leyser, 102. Max Mills, 53. Aaron Norman, 7. Fritz Prenzel, 106, 128. H. Reinhard, 61. L. Robinson, 1, 11, 66, 90, 91. Courtesy of San Diego Zoo, 47, 57, 65, 67, 108, 110, 112, 118. Brian Seed, 35. V. Serbin, 115. Tony Silva, 42. Louise Van der Meid, 20, 51, 54. R.A. Vowles, 59. M.M. Vriends, 19, 60, 86. Courtesy of Vogelpark Walsrode, 2–3, 10, 14–15, 30–31, 36, 45, 46, 49, 50, 55, 56, 62, 69, 74, 75, 76, 78, 80, 82, 84, 85, 88, 89, 98, 99, 103, 107, 109, 111, 113, 119, 120.

A COMPLETE INTRODUCTION TO

PARROTS

COMPLETELY ILLUSTRATED IN FULL COLOR

A grouping of different species of Macaw.

Duke of Bedford

Based on *Parrots and Parrot-like Birds*

© **1987 by T.F.H. Publications, Inc.**

Distributed in the UNITED STATES by T.F.H. Publications, Inc., 211 West Sylvania Avenue, Neptune City, NJ 07753; in CANADA to the Pet Trade by H & L Pet Supplies Inc., 27 Kingston Crescent, Kitchener, Ontario N2B 2T6; Rolf C. Hagen Ltd., 3225 Sartelon Street, Montreal 382 Quebec; in CANADA to the Book Trade by Macmillan of Canada (A Division of Canada Publishing Corporation), 164 Commander Boulevard, Agincourt, Ontario M1S 3C7; in ENGLAND by T.F.H. Publications Limited, 4 Kier Park, Ascot, Berkshire SL5 7DS; in AUSTRALIA AND THE SOUTH PACIFIC by T.F.H. (Australia) Pty. Ltd., Box 149, Brookvale 2100 N.S.W., Australia; in NEW ZEALAND by Ross Haines & Son, Ltd., 18 Monmouth Street, Grey Lynn, Auckland 2 New Zealand; in SINGAPORE AND MALAYSIA by MPH Distributors (S) Pte., Ltd., 601 Sims Drive, #03/07/21, Singapore 1438; in the PHILIPPINES by Bio-Research, 5 Lippay Street, San Lorenzo Village, Makati Rizal; in SOUTH AFRICA by Multipet Pty. Ltd., 30 Turners Avenue, Durban 4001. Published by T.F.H. Publications Inc. Manufactured in the United States of America by T.F.H. Publications, Inc.

Contents

Introduction

The parrot family has occupied a deservedly high place in the favour of bird-keepers ever since the days when the Romans began to import from the East, Plumheaded and Ringnecked, or Alexandrine, Parakeets. The intelligence of parrots and their affection for their owners, their power of imitating the human voice, their longevity and gorgeous plumage, all combine to place them in the front rank as pets or aviary inmates. Some critics, it is true, argue that the colouring of psittacine birds is gaudy rather than beautiful, that their natural cries are disagreeable, that they are destructive to growing plants, and that they are unpleasant to handle without strong gloves; but we may reply that there are some species to which none of these objections apply and many to which only one or two can be made.

A pair of rare Orange Breasted Fig Parrots (Opopsitta gulielmiterti suavissima); top bird is male.

*The Turquoisine Parrot (*Neophema pulchella*) although uncommon in the wild is widely bred in captivity.*

As compared with the science of breeding and managing domestic animals, aviculture is as yet in its infancy; much ignorance still prevails and a good many foreign birds in confinement are subjected to unnecessary suffering through the lack of knowledge and thoughtlessness of their owners. Parrots are no exception, and it is in order to remedy this state of affairs, as well as to increase the pleasure which may be derived from the study of a fascinating group, that this book has been written. It will, perhaps, serve as one of the milestones which mark the road of avicultural progress.

To prevent disappointment and confusion it may be well to add that "Parrots and Parrot-like Birds" is not a complete monograph of the family, but only an attempt to include the majority of those species that have been imported or kept in confinement. Many species and a few sub-genera are not mentioned at all. Of these several are very unlikely to be imported alive by reason of their extreme delicacy in confinement; others, however, we may hope some day to see in our aviaries.

The writer has made use, as far as possible, of the most recent scientific nomenclature. While this may result in many well-known birds appearing under strange and unfamiliar Latin names, modern classification has at least this merit from an avicultural point of view: that it tends to associate in the same sub-genus only birds that are exceedingly closely allied. The reader will therefore be fairly safe in assuming that when little information is given about a rarely imported species it will, in habits, disposition and requirements, be almost identical with better-known and more fully described birds bearing the same sub-generic title.

11

Cages and Aviaries

The average parrot cage would appear to be constructed with the express object of causing the maximum degree of discomfort to the parrot and of inconvenience to its owner. In the first place it is almost invariably at least half the size it should be for the bird it is expected to contain. It is now, I believe, the law of the land that no bird, except when on a railway journey or at a show, may be kept in a cage which does not allow it freely to stretch its wings. From the protection of this beneficient law it would appear that, for some unknown reason, parrots are exempt. Up and down the country one meets with hundreds of parrots in cages so small that they cannot possibly flap their extended wings; yet no parrot

Choose a cage large enough to allow the parrot ample room.

cage is admissable which does not permit this form of exercise to the inmate. A very large and lucrative trade is done by dealers who sell a parrot and cage at "attractive" prices. The cage on these occasions is always far too small, for the provision of a decent-sized cage would eat up the margin of profit. Owing to its cramped environment, the parrot's days are considerably shortened; the owner, therefore, has to buy a new parrot. This is good for the bird trade, but bad for the unhappy birds.

A parrot cage is usually fitted with a swing at the top and a metal grating at the bottom. The former gets in the way of the bird's head when it is sitting on the perch and prevents its flapping its wings; the latter prevents its resting its feet on the flat surface of the cage bottom and collects quantities of dirt, materially increasing the trouble of cleaning the cage. Both these stupid devices should be removed at once.

The tray at the bottom of the average parrot cage is made of very thin metal covered with a thin coat of white enamel. The first time the cage is washed the enamel begins to come off the bottom, exposing the metal, which is specially chosen for its liability to rust. In a very short time it has rusted right through and can then be replaced by a serviceable tray of very solid metal, which will neither rust nor split at the corners. The tray at the bottom of a parrot cage should be thickly covered with gritty sand—sea-sand is excellent when obtainable. If, as most people do, you sand the tray as sparingly as though you were sprinkling gold dust, there will tend to be an unpleasant smell from the unabsorbed moisture of the droppings, the bird's feet will constantly be fouled and the difficulty of cleaning the tray will be much increased, as the droppings will adhere firmly to the metal and solidify.

A parrot's cage should not be covered with a cloth at night.

A caged parrot, in addition to food and drinking water, should be frequently supplied with a small bit of turf, a small twiggy branch of any non-poisonous deciduous tree—oak, ash, elm, lime, beech, hazel, etc.—to bite up, and with a bath. The latter should be fairly shallow, too heavy for the bird to tip over, easy to step into, not too slippery, and of sufficient size. It should be placed, if possible, in such a position that the droppings from the perch fall clear of it. If a parrot is slow in taking an interest in turf, twigs, bath, or for that matter any kind of food that would be beneficial to it, do not be discouraged, but continue to offer them at regular intervals, for months if need be. Sooner or later they are pretty sure to be patronized. It took me nearly two years to induce my Bourke's Parrakeets to partake of any green stuff.

Many parrots which do not bathe freely love to be stood out in a shower of warm rain, or, in winter, to be sprayed with tepid water. But never force a shower bath on a bird that not only objects to the first few drops that fall on it, but continues to object after a minute has passed.

The only really effective way of disinfecting a parrot cage is to scorch every part of it with the flame of a blowtorch. You can never quite trust disinfectants to do their work.

A rectangular cage two feet ten inches long, two feet wide, and one foot eight inches high of

wire netting on a good solid metal frame with an equally substantial metal tray at the bottom is useful for newly-arrived parakeets, as it allows them a certain amount of wing exercise. Put the perch as near to one end of the cage as will permit the bird's tail just to

Check the spacing between bars, some species may be able to squeeze through widely-spaced bars.

clear the wire when it is sitting with its back towards it. That will leave a foot or two of flying space from the perch to the wire of the further end. With delicate birds it is a good thing to have a sheet of zinc to hook on to the back and ends of the cage to keep off draughts. The sand tray must be fairly substantial and of a good fit.

Nothing is more maddening than trying to push a tray that has buckled out of shape and split at the corners in or out of a cage containing a nervous bird. If the parakeets in the cage are small, be careful, when you are cleaning, to stop up the space where the tray goes in; otherwise you will return to find them loose in the birdroom, or, if a window or door be open, in the garden.

Never put any kind of paint or varnish on any parrot cage or aviary, or the birds will nibble it and get poisoned. Creosote, when dry, is, however, a safe dressing for woodwork.

Cages and Aviaries

There are two types of outdoor aviaries which can be considered really satisfactory—movable aviaries and fixed ones with the floor, both of shelter and flight, made of brick, concrete, or similar hard material which is as easily washed and disinfected as the floor of a well-made dog kennel. The usual type of outdoor aviary—a fixed one with an earthen floor to the flight—is a disease-trap which gets steadily more destructive the longer it stands. No experienced pheasant breeder would think of trying to rear his stock year after year in the same run, yet far more delicate birds are treated as though they were immune from the harmful effects of stale ground. Of course, if you like, you can keep such an aviary filled by buying six times as many birds of a certain species as you would need to do if you housed your first pair in a healthy fashion so that there was no need to constantly replace casualties; or, when the ground becomes "sick" to one species, you can try new ones that for a time do not suffer so much. But this is hardly good

aviculture, nor even particularly humane treatment of animals. Re-turfing and disinfecting the ground with lime may be a palliative to the evils of a fixed site, but in practice I have found it a poor one.

A rectangular movable aviary, twenty-four feet by eight feet by eight feet, gives very good breeding results with parakeets not larger than a King and also with the smaller cockatoos. The aviary, including the whole of the floor, is covered with strong half-inch mesh wire netting and the wooden framework of the flight is on the outside of the wire and not on the inside. The object of covering the floor is to exclude rats and other burrowing animals. Grass quickly grows through the meshes and makes the wire invisible. Young mice can get through even half-inch mesh, but full grown ones have difficulty in doing so and frequently share the fate of the vegetarian weasel in

An aviary partitioned into a row of flights.

the fable which entered a barn by a small hole when he was thin and found egress impossible when he had fattened on the farmer's store. The advantage of having the wooden framework on the outside is that the birds cannot bite it, nor can they sit on it and soil it with their droppings.

In the top left-hand corner of the aviary flight is a small hinged door that opens inward and upward. This door can be propped open at any time when it is desired to set a bird at liberty; it should have a fastening on the outside as well as on the inside or a playful bird may undo and open it. The same door is used when the catching box is brought into operation. This catching box is a rectangular box of wire netting two feet six inches by one foot six inches with an inside lining of taut string netting to keep the birds from knocking themselves against the wire and hurting their heads and nostrils. It is made to hook to the top of the aviary in front of the small top corner door and it is itself fitted with a wooden door, corresponding in size to the aperture of the top door, which slides in a groove from left to right. When you desire to catch a bird, hook the catching box onto the aviary, push back the slide of the catching box, undo the fastenings of the little top door, and tie one end of a longish bit of string round the base of the top door (the top door should be of wire on a wooden frame). Pass the other end of the string through a mesh of the wire in the aviary roof so as to supply leverage for pulling the top door open against the roof of the aviary. Then take your stand about half way back in the aviary flight, still holding the string in your hand, and then either yourself, or with the help of an assistant, gently drive the bird you wish to capture into the catching box. As soon as it enters the box, slacken the string you are holding and the top door, if properly oiled and working freely, as it should be before you start operations, falls downward of its own weight, making the bird a prisoner. You then mount a pair of steps, push forward and fasten the slide of the catching box, close and fasten the top door,

and the capture is safely effected without any chasing about with a net. It is very important in the hurry of the moment, not to forget the catching box slide. If you do, as soon as you unhook the catching box the bird darts out to freedom and the catching has to be done over again—under much more difficult circumstances! Of course a very wary bird may refuse to enter the catching box, especially if it has been caught in

inches by two feet six inches. In the centre of the front of the aviary flight, three feet six inches above the ground, is a small door one foot two inches by one foot; just inside this door and practically on a level with it is a metal bracket holding the bath and fruit dish, and when necessary, a seed dish as well.

The wire roof at the front end of the aviary flight is covered with corrugated metal to give some

In a community aviary numerous perches forestall squabbling.

it before; in that case, other methods have to be adopted. When a net is used, always cover the rim with thick, soft padding.

In the bottom left-hand corner of the front of the aviary flight is an entrance door four feet six

protection from sun and rain, and further protection is afforded by other sheets of corrugated metal which cover the shelter and project about two feet over the shelter end of the flight.

In addition, a flat circular piece of wood four feet in diameter is fixed on the outside of the centre of the wire roof of the aviary flight. Four perches diverging to the four corners of the aviary

flight are fastened at one end to a stout piece of wood being attached to the circular shelter disc above, as the stalk of a mushroom is attached to the umbrella portion. The other end of the left-hand front perch runs up to the bottom end of the little top door in the left-hand corner, thus leading a bird up to the catching box when the door is open.

The aviary shelter itself is two feet six inches deep from back to front and the same height as the flight. In the centre of the front of

An indoor flight equipped with a safety porch to prevent the escape of birds.

the shelter, eleven inches from the top, is a window one foot eight inches long and one foot high. In the righthand corner, ten inches from the top and nine and one-half inches from the side, is a circular entrance hole five inches in diameter. This entrance can be closed by a down-dropping slide eight inches by six and one-half inches, which runs in a groove and is raised by a twenty-five foot length of picture wire running through brass screw-eyes and a pulley at either right-angle bend. The wire terminates in a length of cord, and a loop is made in the cord to slip over a check on the outside of the front of the flight when the slide is pulled up. In addition to the large window in the front, the shelter has four other small windows eight and one-half inches by six and one-half inches, covered with wire netting on the inside, as are the whole of the back and two sides of the shelter. Two of these windows are in the sides of the shelter seven inches from the top; one is exactly opposite the entrance hole so that its light may encourage a bird to pass through and the other is in the same relative position on the other side of the back of the flight. In the right-hand side of the shelter is a small door one foot square on the inside of which is fixed a stout bit of wire to hold the seed dish and another to hold a small receptacle for water

A flight enclosed by wire mesh communicates with a solidly enclosed shelter via a flap door.

which is only needed when birds are confined to the shelter and have not access to the bath in the flight.

The shelter has three perches one foot six inches from the top, running from back to front and so arranged that no droppings fall into the seed dish. One of these perches leads up to the entrance hole and a corresponding perch in the flight also leads up to the entrance hole, care being taken to fasten the ends of the perches as close as possible to the lower edge of the entrance hole, so that birds do not have to jump up and jump down when passing through.

The floor of the shelter should be of metal and sufficiently strong for the person cleaning out the aviary to tread on it without causing damage. It should be thickly covered with dry sand. On no account use damp sand, as this is liable to cause chills.

The roof of the shelter should be made waterproof and mouseproof with corrugated metal on top. The corrugated metal should project somewhat into the flight so as to overhang the cross perch in the flight, already mentioned as being nine inches from the front of the aviary shelter. The aviary shelter itself

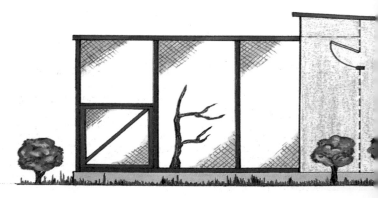

Above: *Corrugated roofing over a section of this aviary provides a protected area.*

should always be boarded with tongue-and-grooved lumber. Where hard-biting birds are kept, such as the bigger broadtails, Ringnecks, and parrots, the woodwork of the front of the aviary shelter must be covered with wire netting, but for the smaller broadtails and Asiatic parakeets, lovebirds, etc., this is unnecessary. In the case of cockatoos, pileated parakeets, and other hard-biting birds, an inner layer of very strong wire netting of the thickest possible gauge must be used throughout the aviary inside the fine mesh wire netting, an outer covering of which is required to exclude mice.

Aviary Management

With accommodation of the type described in the last chapter, even a very large collection of forty or fifty aviaries, containing as many breeding pairs, is easily managed and for the greater part of the year involves but little labour.

First thing in the morning the aviary attendant goes 'round pulling up the slides if the birds have been shut into the shelters for the night. He then takes a box of mixed seed on his arm (with through the night in health and safety.

After breakfast he goes along the front of the aviaries with a can of water and a supply of apples, opens each little front door communicating with the bath and fruit dish bracket, tips the contents of the bath, if clean, into the fruit dish to wash it out, and refills the bath. When the watering is finished, he shuts one pair of birds into the flight by dropping the slide, opens the door at the

Many parrot breeders prefer to prepare a mixture of seeds tailored to the needs of their species.

two or more divisions, if two or more seed mixtures are in use), unlocks the little side door of each aviary shelter and replenishes the food dish, at the same time carefully observing the birds to which the aviary belongs to see that they have come back of the shelter, and cleans the interior. When the interior of the shelter has been thoroughly cleaned with the aid of a non-poisonous disinfectant, the seed dish is also taken out, washed, and refilled with fresh seed. When the shelter is finished, the attendant goes 'round to the front of the flight, pulls up the slide to re-admit the birds to the shelter, gathers a bunch of twiggy branches of some non-poisonous,

A balanced mix of seed, fruit and vegetables necessary for the healthy feeding of many species of parrots.

deciduous tree that the birds enjoy nibbling, ties it up in the flight, and removes any old sticks that may be left from last time. Since the birds occupy only the aviary shelter to a great extent at night, it is usually sufficient to clean one shelter a day in rotation, unless a bird has fallen ill. In which case it is prudent to clean and disinfect the shelter at once, even if it be out of its turn. When the cleaning of the shelter is finished, the work for the day, apart from looking the birds over, is normally ended unless there are heaters to be attended to. In the right-hand bottom corner of each aviary shelter, three feet six inches from the ground, is a wooden box with zinc top; a door one foot two inches by ten inches at the left-hand end; an open wire front facing inwards and separating the interior of the box from the interior of the aviary shelter. In the box is placed any brooder lamp or other heating apparatus which experience has proven to be safe and which will neither produce fumes nor cause an outbreak of fire.

The zinc top of the heater box should have an air space of one inch separating it from the outer wooden top so that if it becomes too hot it will not char or set fire to the wood. In mild climates, no heating provision may be necessary, but in districts where the winter is very severe, some form of electric heating servicing the entire range of aviaries which will, of course, be on a fixed site will have to be installed.

For very large parakeets, such as Red Shinings, a twenty-four foot aviary may not be long enough to provide the wing exercise necessary to secure fertility in the cocks. An extension of twenty feet may be made to the end of the flight, detachable from the rest, for a forty foot aviary would be too long and cumbersome to move in one piece.

Where a number of cock Barrabands and Rock Peplars are kept as day-liberty birds, a communication passage of wire netting three feet nine inches by two feet by one foot nine inches may be constructed to join two or more aviary flights together, but it is advisable to have some means of closing these passages by a sliding partition pulled by a string from the end of the aviary in case any birds behave in a tiresome fashion and dodge to and fro when you want to shut them into the shelters for the night. The shelters themselves, in order to accommodate more birds in comfort and without quarreling, should be about a foot wider than the ordinary ones and should have a few extra perches.

When the aviaries are to be moved onto fresh ground, the grass at the bottom must first be cut and torn up so as to free the wire bottom. This is a rather dirty and tedious job and a pair of canvas gloves is desirable, as well as a flat board to kneel on. When the wire is quite free of the ground, the aviary is raised on wooden rollers ten feet long and seven inches in diameter by the

*Plum-headed Parakeets (*Psittacula cyanocephala*) housed in a permanent brick and mortar construction.*

Skeletal anatomy of the parrot: the bones associated with the limbs are colored blue.

aid of blocks and crowbars and is slid forward onto a fresh site. Four handy men can move a twenty-four foot aviary bodily with tolerable ease and as it is unnecessary to enter the aviary during the actual process of moving, the birds are not unduly alarmed. The use of blocks and tackle would probably facilitate the process even more. October is the best month to begin moving. If the vacated site is ever to be occupied again, it should receive a good dressing of lime and agricultural salt. The former improves the quality of the herbage by making the droppings assimilable as plant food. The salt acts as a useful soil disinfectant. Lime as a disinfectant is perfectly useless and is never to be relied on to destroy germs or parasitic worms.

When a bird dies of an infectious complaint, such as

tuberculosis, the whole of the aviary should be scorched with a blowtorch, particular attention being paid to the wire bottom and sand trays. The perches should be burned and the woodwork re-creosoted. The aviary should be moved onto a fresh site and the vacated site given a very heavy dressing of salt—heavy enough to kill temporarily the grass completely. When rain has washed the salt sufficiently far into the ground for it to be no longer injurious to plant life, the ground may be re-seeded with rye grass.

The time of moving is also a good opportunity to give the outside woodwork of the aviary and particularly the bottom frame

An aviary intended for small species and suited only to warm climates.

a dressing with creosote. Do not put wet creosote where the birds are likely to stain their plumage, and be careful to keep it off the wire, for creosote on wire netting remains wet and sticky for weeks. Ordinary workmen are often very careless in this matter.

While I do not advise a smaller aviary than a twenty-four foot by eight foot by eight foot, one for breeding young of the medium-sized parakeets of a quality equal to their wild parents, it is possible to keep birds for a good number of years in excellent plumage in much smaller and consequently less expensive quarters. They may even breed, anyhow for the first few seasons, but their offspring should not be sold at the price of imported birds.

It is very unfair to ask a fellow aviculturist a biggish price for birds which may look all right, but will only be a source of vexation

and loss as breeders by reason of their lack of stamina, the cocks proving infertile and the hens getting egg-bound, or at best producing nothing but weak and deformed young.

These degenerate birds, bred in very small aviaries, are best

Aviaries built on hilltops allow a natural drainage of rain water.

these applications it is easy to make a satisfactory selection and you have the pleasure of knowing that not only have the birds gone to a place where they will be cared for as priceless treasures, but you have given great joy and interest to a bird lover in a less fortunate position than yourself.

Any bird can be disposed of in this manner, no matter how common, uninteresting, or even defective, and it is a thousand

given away as pets to people who cannot afford to buy parakeets. If a letter be sent to some well-known fanciers' paper offering to give the birds to a good home and stating their needs and also their drawbacks, a very large number of applications will be received—so large, in fact, that it is wise to stipulate that no telegrams nor stamped envelopes be sent and no replies expected by unsuccessful applicants. From

times better to send it where it will be really appreciated than to bestow it on some rather unenthusiastic friend or neighbour, or worse still, dump it at a zoo where it is even less welcome. When the bird is despatched, full directions as to its treatment should be sent with it; in this way sound knowledge as to correct management can be extended—a very desirable thing in an age when people still exist who think it may be right to slit a parrot's tongue in order to encourage it to talk!

Where lack of space or the unevenness of the ground makes it impossible to put up movable aviaries, there is nothing for it but to erect fixed ones with a concrete or tiled floor. In the hard material a hole should be left so that the nesting tree trunk can

A double row of flights along a service corridor.

stand on earth and if there is any risk of rats finding their way up through the hole it can be covered with wire netting. It is most important that the floor of a fixed aviary have a slight slope and a drainage trench which runs off all rainwater immediately. If it collects in pools at the middle or at the sides, the birds will constantly be drinking water fouled by their own droppings.

The shelter should contain as little unnecessary lumber as possible so that it can easily be cleaned and disinfected. Be careful to see that the partition between aviary compartments does not allow birds to damage each other by fighting through the wire. Two large parakeets cannot do much harm to each other through half-inch mesh, but it is dangerous to put a small-beaked species next to a large, quarrelsome neighbour. I once had the upper mandible of a fine cock Hooded Parakeet completely torn off by a Barnard fighting him through half-inch wire. Two Barnards could not have got a grip on each other, but the Hooded's slender beak went right through the mesh. Double wire partitions are therefore essential to protect beaks and toes.

When birds are kept in a fixed aviary it is a good plan to keep a large tray of fresh turf in the flight and another of earth on which oats are thrown to sprout. Green food must also be provided. This, either in cage or aviary, should have its stalks pushed firmly into a vessel of water that is not easily upset. In this way it keeps fresh much longer.

When new birds are turned into an aviary for the first time, keep them shut into the shelter for a few days until they become used to it and know where to find the food. Some species are at first very stupid and obstinate about allowing themselves to be

Sun conures in an outdoor aviary.

close the door of the flight properly behind you. I once lost a Bourke's Parrakeet through neglect of this precaution.

A collection of birds should be looked over carefully after

driven into the shelter for the night. For very difficult cases it is well to keep in readiness a wing of netting on a wooden frame which can be hooked onto the wire mesh of the top of the aviary flight so as to form a blind alley leading up to the entrance hole into the shelter. This will make it less easy for them to keep on breaking back towards the front of the flight. Shutting up can be left until a quarter of an hour before sunset, but when you have new birds allow ample time for getting them in in case they give trouble. Never leave shutting up until it is getting dark as the birds are then apt to knock themselves about if disturbed. Never, also, when driving birds in, forget to

daybreak and at 2:30 p.m. in winter, and after daybreak and at 5:30 p.m. in summer, to see if they are showing signs of incipient illness. Never leave a bird that is showing signs of illness, however slight, where it is until the following day. If you do, it will certainly be dead or dying next morning. With sick birds a stitch in time saves not nine, but ninety-nine. When a bird has recovered from an illness, never return it to exactly the same surroundings in no better condition than it was in when it fell ill; if you do it is sure to get ill again. Either wait till it is in better health, or give it more protection.

A parrot when ill partly closes its eyes and usually, though not invariably, ruffles its feathers and is inclined to put its head "under its wing." A bird which sits with its head "under its wing" and both feet on the perch is practically always ill, but if it has one foot tucked up it is only sleepy. A sick bird has the lower breast and abdomen more puffed than a sleepy one.

An ill bird sits with its "head under a wing" and its feathers ruffled.

has one that cocks its head sideways to look at an object above or below it. Vomiting is a common sign of chill. The action is quite different from that of a bird in breeding condition bringing up food from its crop and either re-swallowing it or feeding its toes, the end of the perch, or its owner. When a parrot vomits, it allows the food to run from the beak onto the ground, or gets rid of it with a shake of the head and the head feathers usually get more or less

Some birds when dozing may be seen to ruffle up a lot on the back and wings, but if the feathers of the breast and belly are fully tight, probably all is well. A bird that stretches itself has seldom much the matter; neither

messed up. Occasionally a parakeet will vomit to get rid of some objectionable substance in the crop without being really unwell, but in ninety-nine cases out of a hundred vomiting means a chill.

Newly-imported birds, are, of course, usually very sensitive to cold and sudden changes of temperature, but do not forget that the main cause of illness in acclimatized birds, i.e., those which have had a complete moult in an outdoor aviary, is not cold and wet but weather, or other conditions, which favour the rapid multiplication of, and assumption of, a virulent nature by bacteria inimical to birds. You may, therefore, expect the largest number of cases of sickness during the summer and autumn and during mild spells in winter. Periods of extreme cold and wet may lower the birds' vitality but they are even harder on our enemy, the microbe, so during the most inclement winter weather, if the birds are reasonably housed and fed, there is seldom any sickness among acclimatized

As with other animals, care must be taken to provide adequate warmth during transport.

stock. For the same reason, large and sudden drops in temperature are more dangerous in relatively high temperatures than in relatively low ones. A drop from eighty-six degrees Fahrenheit to fifty-five degrees is more likely to produce casualties than a drop from fifty-five degrees to twenty-five degrees.

When looking birds over, never make the mistake of not troubling to get a sight of some individual because it has always seemed so robust that you are sure no illness could possibly overtake it. More than once I have lost an old favourite, which has braved the storms of many winters, through rashly assuming, on a lovely June day, that it could not possibly have got ill and must only be in the shelter feeding.

Birds are very regular in their habits and tend to do the same thing at the same time in the same way. An observant bird keeper soon gets to know the ways of each individual in his collection and any deviation from its normal custom should at once

Orange-fronted Conures unavoidably overcrowded during transport.

be enquired into as a possible indication of sickness. Do not make up explanations in your head as to why that bird was not in its accustomed place or flew from an unusual corner. Look for them.

An indispensable adjunct to any large collection is a hospital room where the temperature can be maintained at an even eighty-five degrees even in the coldest weather. The hospital need not be large, as it will not have to accommodate any great number of birds at one time, but it must be well-insulated so as to be as little affected as possible by the outside temperature. If it is a wooden building, it must have double boards with a sawdust-filled space between and double windows. Vita-glass is to be preferred for all hospital, birdroom, and aviary shelter windows.

For heating hospital or birdroom, nothing equals thermostatically controlled electricity, which has only one serious drawback—that of being at times rather expensive. There are various makes of electric heaters which are movable and can be placed beside a sick bird's cage in such a way that it can have a nice choice of temperature. If it wishes to sit on a perch close to the side of the cage nearest to the heater it can enjoy an even temperature of nearly ninety degrees, or it can move away, if the cage is not too small, to a temperature of eighty degrees or less. If you have a very valuable bird very dangerously ill, such an arrangement is of priceless advantage. The vagaries

bird and before morning, if you do not get up two or three times in the night to attend to it, it will be dangerously low and your patient will be in extremis. Gas heating is not quite so bad, but unless you can by some means prevent the fumes getting into the room, your whole collection may be asphyxiated.

If you cannot afford a proper hospital, you may be able inside a room to construct something of boards and glass which will hold a cage or cages, and which can be kept at an even eighty-five degrees by means of one or more of the heaters already referred to as being useful for warming an aviary shelter. Hospital cages for sick birds are also sometimes on the market. If you decide to dispense with all high-temperature appliances and make use of the kitchen or the greenhouse with its immense variation of temperature, you will lose about three-quarters of your sick birds instead of saving about three-quarters.

of all forms of heating dependent on stove or furnace are in such circumstances maddening. No stove or furnace (oil stoves excepted) can be trusted to keep an even temperature for more than five hours without attention. In the evening it will half roast the

In this shipping box ventilation is provided through wire mesh.

Another indispensable adjunct to a collection is a quarantine room, also well heated, where new arrivals can be kept for at least two weeks to make sure they are not suffering from some dangerous infectious ailment. You may neglect the precaution for months or even years without

A group of Rose-ringed Parakeets in a holding flight awaiting transport.

days later she developed septic fever of the most virulent type. Not only did every bird which was at all susceptible to the disease in that enclosure die, but full-winged liberty birds that occasionally came in to feed also caught the infection and spread it about the garden. I lost every King, Crimson-wing, Redrump, Blue Bonnet, Grass Parrakeet, and Many-colour in my collection, and I could never from that day onward, for years after, keep any of the four last mentioned species

mishap, but sooner or later you will regret it.

Many years ago at my old home, I received an apparently healthy Bauer's Parakeet and turned her with a cut wing into a small walled garden. About four

either in cage, aviary, or at liberty, without their falling victims before many months had passed.

Birdrooms necessarily vary enormously in size, shape, and arrangement; but a good birdroom should always be easy

Parrots, like these Golden Conures, benefit from natural perches to gnaw on.

to keep scrupulously clean and should be very light. It should get plenty of winter sun, but should have arrangements for shading in summer, as parrots hate very hot sunshine and often fall victims to sunstroke if unable to escape it. Apart from perches, the less wood and the more metal there is about the structure of a birdroom, the better. Natural perches are best for flight cages and they can be removed and burned as they get dirty or worn out. Do not crowd a flight cage with too many perches, but allow the birds the maximum of room for wing exercise. An even temperature in a birdroom is very desirable. We hear a lot about birds being able to stand cold at night because even in the tropics the nights are very chilly, but all I know is that if you allow this sort of tropic night to be produced in your birdroom you are likely to be the possessor of a good many corpses.

If a bird accidentally escapes, the first thing to do is to put food on the top of the aviary or aviaries gradually work the food under or into some sort of trap and a capture will soon be accomplished. If you locate the stray at some distance, go in pursuit of it with a trap feeding

If escape is a possibility, ensure that the bird cannot travel far (usually accomplished by trimming wing feathers).

it is most likely to visit, and to keep the whole place as quiet and free from disturbance as you can until it has come down and fed. A bird that has found your artificial food after escaping is already more than half caught. You can tray and a decoy—its mate for choice. A very good form of trap feeding tray consists of a kind of hinged dish-cover arrangement of wire netting two feet nine inches by two feet three inches and one foot three inches high at the apex, and provided with an inner lining of taut string netting one and one-half inches from the wire, to prevent the bird hurting its head should it fly up in alarm as the trap falls. The dish-cover part is propped up on a short bit of stick to which a long line is attached and well inside is placed a dish of seed containing no peanuts.

When you set the trap close to the decoy's cage be careful to see that the prop pulls away easily and the trap falls quickly. A hanging fall of the trap may alarm the bird and it may get caught and severely injured by the descending rim as it tries to escape. The shorter the stick the quicker, and consequently the safer the fall, so the trap should be propped up no higher than is necessary to allow the bird to enter. Do not pull the moment the bird is inside, but wait till it settles to feed and is unsuspicious. In the front of the dish-cover part of the trap is a small door of just sufficient size to admit the arm through which the bird can be driven into a cage or caught by hand.

If you intend to keep birds at liberty, send a courteous note to neighbours whose property they are likely to visit, asking them to use their influence to prevent their being shot. A similar notice in the local paper is also desirable. There are, unfortunately, a good many persons about who will shoot a strange bird to find out what it is, or in mistake for a hawk; but very few are so utterly lacking in good feeling as to shoot a neighbour's pet bird knowing that it belongs to him. People who get their birds shot have often only themselves to thank for neglecting to make it widely known that they keep foreign birds at liberty.

Never let your birds be a nuisance to your neighbours, but keep fruit-eating species and fruit bud-eating species shut up at those seasons of the year when they are inclined to be mischievous. If damage is done,

compensate liberally.

Keep also on good terms with the children and youths of the district and when you send a subscription to Scouts, Guides, football teams, etc., ask that they will do you a good turn by using their influence to prevent ignorant

Care should be taken not to harm a bird while retrieving it with a net.

or mischievous persons from injuring your birds.

Never keep quarrelling birds together. There is no greater or commoner form of cruelty which aviculturists indulge in through their greed than to cram as many birds as possible into an aviary. How would they like it, I wonder, if they were confined, without means of escape, with some savage bully who was perpetually seeking to injure or destroy them? If one bird dislikes another sufficiently to fly the whole length of the aviary in order to attack it, those birds should be separated at once.

Vermin, of course have to be dealt with. Mice are always a nuisance, but an aviary of one-half inch mesh netting kept in good repair with a mouse-proof shelter should not give them much chance. If, however, you can obtain an even finer mesh, get it. Rats and weasels can be excluded by seeing that the netting is kept in good repair, particular attention being paid to the floor netting at the time of the annual shift of movable aviaries. For weasels, unbaited tunnel traps of bricks and turf with the trap set in the middle are often effective. Hawks and other predatory birds are at times a

Philippine Hanging Parrot (Loriculus philippensis).

nuisance and though parakeets are usually too wide awake to allow themselves to be caught, a hawk scares them badly and Barrabands frightened by a hawk in the afternoon will sometimes refuse to return to the feeding aviary and roost out, thus exposing themselves to a far more deadly enemy, the owl. Hawks are usually rather punctual and regular in their habits when one is not carrying a gun, appearing at the same time each day and following the same line of flight. When one is armed they are extremely irregular and unpunctual, but now and then they forget and one has one's chance. A very long shot should be taken if a nearer one is not offered and if they take themselves off for good your object is gained. Rooks and Jackdaws occasionally show a disposition to mob cockatoos and large parakeets. A shot or two will teach them to mind their manners for a considerable time. Starlings are a great plague in the breeding season as they occupy every available nest box and nest hole. Some pairs are extremely savage and determined, and I have known them to defeat even such powerful birds as Pennants and Mealy Rosellas when the latter have been trying to nest at liberty. Constant persecution of the starling population with an air rifle or walking-stick gun is the best remedy.

The owner of a collection of foreign birds should cultivate a lively imagination, combined with an ability to foresee coming evils, equal to that of the prophet Jeremiah. Whenever you make any disposition with regard to a bird, always try to think of all the catastrophes that may result in consequence and endeavor to guard against them. There is

One of the color varieties of the Peach-faced lovebird, the so-called blue.

generally just one you have not thought of, but if so, you will remember it next time! In the same way, consider the possible evil effects of any changes in the environment of your birds, for which you are not responsible and, if you can, meet them also. For example, if the temperature drops to twenty degrees below the freezing point in May when you have a valuable hen nesting in a shelter, put in a heater to stop her from getting egg-bound. Do not wait until she gets egg-bound, for even if by treatment you save the bird you will lose the eggs, for a parakeet, once egg-bound, hardly ever sits.

While experience is naturally of the greatest value, it is true to say that good aviary attendants are born and not made. An aviary attendant must possess the gift of being able to detect the very earliest signs of illness; he should be painstaking and clean in his work; it should be possible to trust him to carry out implicitly in one's absence even orders of which he does not himself see the sense. He should possess the prophetic vision of possible evil already alluded to. He should be keen enough on his job to be willing in time of emergency to sacrifice, without being ordered to do so, a Saturday afternoon or Sunday to recapturing a strayed bird, and he should be ready to get up in the middle of a winter night to attend to a sick one because he feels the threatened loss as keenly as the owner.

Sometimes talent appears in very unlikely quarters, quite elderly men who have never had anything to do with foreign birds quickly attain a skill and reliability that is hard to beat.

Women also make good aviary attendants, often showing quickness of observation and great devotion to their charges, coupled with scrupulous care in carrying out instructions.

Aviary Management

The worst possible type of aviary attendant is a lad—particularly a country one. There may be honourable exceptions, but boys present, as a general rule, an almost perfect combination of all the qualities least to be desired. Even people of moderate means who cannot afford a whole-time aviary attendant, but include the care of the aviary with other work, would be very well advised to pay the difference between a man's and a boy's wages in order to secure

Sixteen-day-old Jandaya Conure.

someone who will discharge all his duties with far more intelligence, trustworthiness, and care than the average youngster.

Occasionally circumstances compel one to take charge of nestling birds which have not yet fed themselves. If young enough to have no fear and open their beaks for food, the larger species may be reared as recommended in the article on Rock Peplars. The degree of heat supplied must be in proportion to the age and development of the brood. Very tiny babies may need a temperature of eighty-five degrees. Older nestlings which are fledged and have learned the

fear of human beings will usually begin to feed themselves as soon as they get really starving. They should be placed in a box cage in a very warm situation. Blotting paper should be substituted for sand on the cage floor, as sand gets into the birds' eyes and beaks as they are struggling to get out. The floor of the cage should be sprinkled with well soaked canary and millet seed, shelled soaked sunflower, cracked soaked hemp, and stale brown breadcrumbs almost as fine as powder. The food should be constantly renewed as it gets dry, or is scratched into corners.

If the young bird is growing dangerously weak, or appears to have caught a chill, forced feeding must be resorted to. For emergencies of this kind, there is nothing better than a raw egg beaten up in half a cupful of new milk and administered, a drop at a time, from the end of a small camel-hair paintbrush. Wrap the bird in a handkerchief and hold it gently but firmly in the left hand, the first finger and thumb keeping its head as steady as possible. Place the drop of milk at the side of the upper mandible, near the lower edge, and towards the tip. If it keeps its beak firmly closed you will need an assistant to hold the bird while you open its beak and administer the food in very small quantities at a time. Do not give more than three or four drops at the first feeding, as too much milk given before a bird is used to it, is liable to induce vomiting, and it is better to give a little which is kept down than a larger quantity which reappears. As soon as possible mix some whole wheat, rye, or a dark bread with the milk and get the bird onto a more natural and less liquid diet.

Take great care not to mess

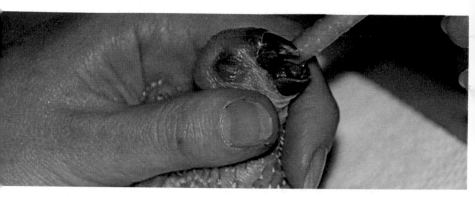

An eyedropper being used to raise a twelve-day-old Nanday chick.

the bird's plumage, either with the milk or with the perspiration from your hand, as a bird with its feathers messed up is liable to chill and also feels uncomfortable and wretched. A meal should be given not less than once in three hours and if possible once or twice during the night if the patient is in a weak state. As soon as it starts to eat seed or breadcrumbs, the milk can be soon discontinued, as it is too stimulating for a bird that is well nourished. The young of very small species, even when healthy, are often easier to feed from the tip of a camel-hair paintbrush than from the mouth or fingers, especially when they are only beginning to get used to their human foster parents.

The requirements of parrot-like birds in the matter of nesting accommodation are of so varied a nature that little general advice can be given. It is always, however, wise to have the entrance holes facing north, as some species are very particular that their front door should have this aspect, possibly because it is cooler in tropical countries.

In wild birds what may be termed the mental factor is often almost as important as the physical, where the success in breeding is to be achieved. A nest that takes a hen's fancy is a powerful incentive to her to lay and conversely the lack of an attractive nest is likely to keep her from laying, even if by good management her reproductive organs have been brought into a state of pronounced activity.

It is a good sign if, very soon after the nest is put in, the hen is seen to go right inside, although it may only be for a few moments.

It is a bad sign if she repeatedly flies off after a hurried glance at the entrance hole; if she pointedly ignores the entrance and for days searches every other part of the nest but the right one for a way in; or if, after showing some interest in the nest for the first few days, her visits of inspection grow steadily fewer and shorter; all these evidences of dissatisfaction should point to the immediate need of providing other types of nest that may prove more attractive. King and Crimsonwing Parakeets like a tremendously deep nest box in which they can climb down from a height of about six feet nearly to ground level. Always, of course, make the interior of a nest climbable by a strip of wire netting tacked to the side.

Notes on Breeding

Although there are a few exceptions, most members of the parrot family, when breeding, are very intolerant of the presence of their own and allied species, and each pair must be kept separately.

Most parrot-like birds, also, are unsafe companions for birds of other orders and most use no nesting material, laying their white eggs at the bottom of a hollow in a decayed tree trunk. Nearly all like their nest to be a little on the small side and the entrance hole leading to it to be also rather small, but care must, of course, be taken not to provide boxes so small that the young cannot develop properly and not to provide entrance holes so narrow that birds cannot get through them, especially if they are weak-billed species which cannot enlarge the holes by biting the wood. The interior of nest boxes must be made climbable by tacking a strip of wire netting to the side below the entrance. Although they are rather heavy to move in some cases, natural hollow tree trunks make good and attractive nests, especially for the larger species, such as cockatoos. They can be made a little more easy to handle if they are cut in transverse sections, the sections being fastened together temporarily when the nest has been erected in a suitable position.

Wooden nest boxes are of two kinds; hanging boxes with a wooden bottom; and "grandfather clock" nest boxes seven or more feet in height. These latter have a bottom of fine mesh wire netting to exclude mice and are filled to the necessary height with peat moss, on the top of which a handful or so of soft decayed wood is placed. The bottom of the nest should be, in most cases, about eighteen inches below the entrance hole. In the case of grass parakeets a rather shorter "climb-down" is desirable, while in the case of King and Crimson-wing Parakeets an extremely long climb-down is preferred, the nest being only a few inches above ground level. One reason why so many people find that their Kings and Crimson-wings do not take to the nest box, but prefer to lay on the ground, is that they have not

Cross-section of a nest box showing ladder and inspection hatch.

provided anything like a long enough climb-down. If possible, provide a pair of birds with more than one nest box and give the different boxes different aspects, as some birds like a northerly aspect for the entrance hole and others a southerly one.

Always, if you possibly can, place the nest boxes in the flight and not in the shelter, as young bred in an aviary shelter are far more likely to be rickety. You can provide a little overhead shelter from sun and torrential rain, but a certain amount of rain falling on a nest box does not matter if it has a good lid, especially if it be the grandfather clock type.

Some hen birds, however, do not take kindly to a grandfather clock nest and tend to burrow about too much in the soft material at the bottom, sometimes burying their eggs. Such birds need to be provided with nest boxes with hard wooden bottoms, these bottoms being always concave to prevent the eggs from rolling about.

A few inches above the level of the actual nest it is a good plan to have a little inspection door cut in the side of the box, but the greatest care must be taken that this door cannot get opened accidentally, or be opened by the birds themselves playing with the catch.

If a hen bird apparently in breeding condition does not settle down as she should to a nest box, or, after an initial interest in it, seems later to grow tired of it and to want something different, try, if you can, to meet her fancy by providing other boxes of a different type. With birds the psychological factor is nearly, if not quite, as important, where breeding success is concerned, as the physical factor of good health. A box that takes a

A decayed tree trunk placed in the aviary replicates the site used for nesting in the wild.

hen's often capricious fancy, is a most powerful inducement to her to go to nest. Double brooded parakeets should always be provided with at least two nest boxes of similar type, for many of

41

them have the Budgerigar's habit of laying again before the young of the first round have left the nest, the cock taking sole charge

Two commercially available nesting boxes; some pairs may prefer one entrance hole placement to the other.

of their feeding.

Some cock parakeets, particularly Redrumps and their near allies and certain grass parakeets, such as Turquoisines, very quickly tire of their offspring. The males, especially, must be watched most carefully in case they should turn on their sons and kill them. I have even known a cock Barraband do this though the habit is very rare in members of that sub-genus. The larger broadtails, Rosellas, etc., may also need watching though they do not usually tire of their offspring as quickly as the Redrump family.

Most parrots and cockatoos are tolerant of the presence of their young for a long period after they have left the nest but some breeders have found that in this respect Leadbeater's Cockatoo is an exception.

If young parakeets have to be taken away from their parents at a rather early age, keep them at a comfortably warm temperature and scatter seed, both soaked and dry, all over the floor of the cage. On no account place the seed only in a dish. It is usually the smaller seeds such as canary, that the young of even the larger parakeets will first begin to pick up. A little soft food in the shape of milk-sop made with whole meal bread and mashed up apple may also be offered. This, for cleanliness sake, can be put in a dish; but the birds will take it more readily if at first it is scattered about in little separate pieces instead of being left altogether in a solid mass.

If it should be necessary to hand rear a bird too young to feed itself, a good mixture which suits most species consists of whole meal bread, chewed up and well moistened with raw milk. A little sweet apple also chewed up and a little sweet grape juice may be added. Never on any account give sour fruit. A little yolk of raw egg may also be added to the mixture. Give the food warm, indeed almost hot. It can often be warmed by being placed in a cup put in a larger vessel of almost boiling water. The best implement for administering the food is a camel-hair paintbrush. Put a little of the warm, semi-liquid mash on the brush and then place it gently against the side of the young bird's beak near the tip. When it is hungry it can, with a little patience, soon be induced to begin to feed and once it is feeding freely, meals administered every two or three hours during the day should enable the youngster to be reared successfully. Be careful not to let the young bird's plumage get sticky and messed up, wiping it clean, if need be, with cotton wool dipped in warm water. I have even known miniature bibs used with great success in the hand rearing of a family of young Turquoisines!

Birds which, like certain species of cockatoos, are inveterate wood-biters, sometimes need to have the whole of the outside of their nest box covered with strong-mesh wire netting to prevent them from destroying it.

A type of nest which often appeals to lovebirds and to some of the grass parakeets has a kind of passage approach.

Birds which are rearing young should be very generously fed, especially in the case of the larger species. Rickets is the commonest trouble with young birds of the parrot family of many different species, and there is no more certain way of producing rickets than failing to make due allowance for the large appetites of a growing family. Species which normally should not be given too much hemp or

sunflower seed may sometimes, when they are rearing young, safely be given rather more and it is a good plan at this time, not only to have dry seed in the shelter, but other seed in a clean receptacle in the flight so placed that rain can fall upon it. This

A clutch of Masked Lovebird eggs.

naturally soaked seed should not, however, be left so long that it becomes stale and mouldy. Green food and fruit must also be supplied liberally, together with milk-sop made with whole meal bread and sweetened, which is especially useful for the larger species. When rearing young Amazon parrots successfully a friend of the writer's also offered the parent birds milk-pudding and even boiled white fish, not, of course, of a salty kind.

I have said before that there are certain species of parrot-like birds which do not follow the

Turquoisine Parrot hatchlings and eggs on the concave floor of the nest box.

normal breeding habits of the majority of the members of the family. (Incidentally, it is generally the rule that if the male bird feeds the sitting hen he does not help to incubate the eggs, although he will assist in feeding the young. If, however, as is the case with some of the cockatoos, he takes his turn at incubating, he will not feed the sitting female.)

Most members of the lovebird family line their nest boxes with fine strips of bark, twigs, etc., carried to the nest in the beak in the case of some species, and among the feathers of the rump in the case of others. Liberal supplies of the fresh twigs of such trees as willow and poplar should therefore be provided throughout the breeding season. Lovebirds should also have plenty of spare boxes in their aviary which the young can use as dormitories after they have left the nest in which they have been hatched. It is said that hanging parrots also make use of some fine vegetable material to line their nests and the curious Palm Cockatoo is said to give the nest a lining of small branches and twigs. Even the common Roseate Cockatoo will sometimes go through a pretense of nest building, though this often does not get much further than waving a twig about at the entrance to the nest which is dropped before it is taken inside!

The only parakeet which builds a real nest is the South American Quaker. This relative of the conures should be provided with a large quantity of twigs and some kind of platform corresponding to the natural branches of trees on which the nest can be constructed. The Quaker, or Grey-breasted Parakeet, is an extremely dangerous bird in mixed company, but it does not object to the presence of its own kind, even when breeding.

The Cockatiel is amiable towards birds of other species, but breeding pairs should be kept separate from their own kind. All the parakeets of the Rosella family are dangerously spiteful when in breeding condition and, if a range of breeding aviaries should be put up, care must be taken to see that the partitions are double-wired. If this precaution be neglected the birds will bite off each other's beaks and toes when fighting through the wire. Even the much more gentle grass parakeets must be kept apart from their own kind when breeding.

Some of the smallest lovebirds, such as the Nyassa and Black-cheeked will agree fairly well if allowed to breed on the colony system; but the larger species such as the Masked and Fischer's are best kept separate; and this is absolutely essential in the case of the Peach-faced, which is a most savage and pugnacious bird.

The Red-faced Lovebird, a very shy nester in captivity,

should be tempted, in addition to ordinary nest boxes, by a large block of solid peat hung up in the aviary in which an artificial hole like a rathole is started.

The South American parrotlets are extremely pugnacious when in breeding condition and often at other times, and breeding pairs must always be kept separate. This sub-genus uses no nesting material.

Although cases to the contrary have been reported, Budgerigars will not, as a rule, feed nestlings which, when first hatched, are covered with long

Four-day-old Sulphur-crested Cockatoo.

white down. They therefore make unreliable foster parents for young grass parakeets which are better entrusted to the care of lovebirds if these do not suffer from the common vice of plucking their young.

The eggs of the temperamental and difficult Turquoisine can sometimes profitably be entrusted to the care of Elegants or Bourkes.

Notes on Breeding

As a general rule avoid looking in the nests of parrot-like birds if you have reason to believe that all is well. Pileated parakeets and some lorikeets are especially likely to desert their young if they have reason to suspect that the nest box has been opened. Other species may be much more tolerant of interference, especially as the young get older, but members of the Ringneck family at any stage are best left very strictly alone.

If a case of egg-binding should occur, keep the hen at a temperature of at least eighty-five degrees Fahrenheit until the egg is laid and then allow her a long rest of several weeks before giving her the chance of going to nest again.

Occasionally, young birds leave the nest with only their flight and tail feathers, their bodies being almost completely bare.

Red-faced Lovebirds in the nesting site at thirty days old.

This is due to the fact that they have been plucked by their parent, or parents. Nearly always it is the hen who is the offender, but now and again the cock is also guilty. The cause and cure of this tiresome habit which sometimes, at any rate, seems to be hereditary are at present unknown. It appears most frequently among birds which have been improperly fed and kept short of exercise and amusement, but it can occur in even the best-managed aviaries where the inmates have a great amount of freedom and more or less natural conditions. I have known examples of the vice among broadtailed parakeets, Amazon parrots, lories, lovebirds and Budgerigars, but I have never yet come across a case among parakeets of the Ringneck family, cockatoo or grass parakeets. Sometimes a young hen will pluck her first family and sometimes a hen will take to it later in life when she has reared several broods perfectly. The habit once started may be partially abandoned, but never, in my experience, completely so, and it usually tends to get worse rather than better. As a rule the plucking ceases when the young bird leaves the nest and occasionally a little while before it leaves, but I have known pileated parakeets, which are sometimes extremely bad pluckers, to continue the vice even after their young have flown. As a general rule, if the young birds escape a chill in their naked condition, they grow their plumage rapidly once they have left the nest and soon show no trace of the treatment to which they have been subjected.

Some young birds of the parrot family may leave the nest in a more or less rickety condition, either through some

Three young Masked Lovebirds amid nesting material shredded principally by the hen.

constitutional weakness in the parents, or through the failure of the owner to provide enough food of the right kind. Next to underfeeding, the commonest cause of rickets is putting the nest boxes in the aviary shelter and not in the flight.

I, myself, have found it quite impossible to breed healthy grass parakeets, free from rickets, in indoor flight cages or aviaries, even when every comfort and delicacy in the way of varied green food has been supplied.

In the mildest form of rickets the young birds are unable to fly when they leave the nest, but their feet and legs are quite strong and well-formed and they can walk and climb normally.

Such birds can usually safely be left in the aviary for their parents to attend to and in a few days they will begin to fly, and before very long look perfect in every way, even though their breeding performance when they themselves are adult may not perhaps be all that is desired.

Incidentally, when a brood of young birds is expected to leave the nest, it is a very good plan to tie branches of trees all over both ends of the flight from ground level up to the top, and near the top it is well to provide some overhead and side shelter from wind and rain. The branches should be so shaped and fastened that they project at right-angles to the end of the flight so that they offer comfortable perching accommodation all the way up and an easy means of ascent. A flat branch, tightly tied against the end of the flight, like a

A pair of White-fronted Amazons protecting their eggs in a nest box (12 × 12 × 24" deep).

fan, is very little use to the young birds. As many young parakeets are at first exceedingly wild and nervous and apt to injure themselves by crashing against the wire netting, it is very desirable to have some arrangement, like the one just described, which makes it possible to leave them in peace until they have grown accustomed to the use of their wings and to the sight of human beings.

Nothing is more frightening and nerve-wracking than trying to drive a newly-fledged brood of parakeets, strong and very nervous, into the aviary shelter because the flight is so exposed that it is not safe to leave them there during the night.

Reverting to the problem of rickets, in more severe cases the young birds on first leaving the nest will be found, not only unable to fly, but also practically unable to walk. In this case, it is no use leaving them in the aviary, as the parents will soon give them up as hopeless and proceed to neglect them; and, if it should rain, they

White-fronted Amazon at two weeks old.

Four weeks old

will be unable to find shelter and will become soaked and chilled. They should be placed in a roomy cage for which short turf, frequently changed, makes a good bottom and should be kept really warm. Appropriate seed and food of all kinds should not merely be placed in dishes but scattered over the floor of the cage as well. In most cases young birds will, before long, begin to feed themselves, but if they should show no signs of doing so after many hours have elapsed, hand feeding may have to be resorted to. In time, these rickety cases usually improve to an almost unbelievable degree so that they are quite suitable as pets, or even pleasingly ornamental in an aviary, even though they may never be any good for stock purposes. If the weather is very warm it is beneficial, once they have begun to feed freely, to put them out-of-doors in their cage for a few hours daily so that they can get the benefit of direct sunlight. They should not, however, be exposed to the full glare of the hot summer sun which nearly all parrots dislike intensely.

Six weeks old

Eight weeks old

African Parrots

African Grey Parrot
Psittacus erithacus

Distribution: Equatorial Africa.
Adult male: Ashy grey, paler on
the rump and abdomen. Flight
feathers dark grey. Tail and tail-
coverts red. Bill blackish. Irises
pale yellow. Length thirteen
inches. Size about that of a
pigeon.
Adult female: Similar to the male
but smaller with a less massive
head and beak. The bare skin at
the back of the eye is said to be
more rounded and less elliptical
in shape.
Immature: Differs in having the
tail dark red towards the tip and
the under tail-coverts dark red,
tinged with grey. Irises dark grey.

The Grey Parrot has been a
well-known favourite for a great
number of years, and many
stories are told of its intelligence

*The African Grey Parrot grows to
a length of 13 inches.*

and linguistic powers. It is, par
excellence, the bird for those who
want a house pet to amuse them
with its mimicry of the human
voice. Not only does it adapt itself
wonderfully to cage life, and with
proper treatment survive for an
immense number of years, but as
a talker it has few rivals and no
superior. Moreover, if some of its
whistling cries are unpleasantly
shrill, it never, unless terrified,
can be properly said to screech.
It is also of a more equable
temperament than
the Blue-fronted Amazon. Few
Amazons can be trusted in
moments of mischievous
excitement to refrain from nipping
the fingers of even their best
friends, but a Grey is seldom

treacherous. Once he has really given you his heart—and very often only one person is so honoured—he is always gentle except under great provocation, but anyone, especially a stranger, who is foolish enough to make advances that are not welcome, does so at his own peril and has no reason to complain if, as is extremely likely, he receives a severe bite.

The Grey Parrot should be fed on a seed mixture of two parts canary, one-half part hemp, one part sunflower, one part oats, with plenty of fruit. Sweet, soft fruits like grapes are the most relished, as are ripe pears. Apples are eaten if of the best dessert kinds and in good condition, but a Grey has a very discriminating palate, and usually rejects this fruit if it is soft, sour, or ill-flavored. A very small bit of plain cake does no harm as a tit-bit, but tea, coffee, soaked bread, meat, bones, butter, and milk should never be given. According to one authority, the stupid habit of giving parrots bread and butter and milk is a common cause of the tuberculosis to which they often fall victims, it being claimed that they are susceptible to the bovine as well as to the avian form of the disease. Very young Grey Parrots will sometimes eat only boiled maize (corn), a food which must be prepared fresh daily, but they can usually soon be induced to take soaked seed and, in due course, dry seed. Sunflower soaked until the shell is quite soft is very attractive to young parrots, but the water in which seed is soaking must be changed daily or it will become very offensive.

Grey Parrots are not regular bathers, but appreciate an occasional spray or rain bath. The dry streaky plumage of the numerous unfortunate birds whose owners never allow them to bathe contrasts very unfavourably with the appearance of well-cared-for specimens.

A Grey Parrot should have a

A cleansing shower, of tepid water, may be given without ill effects.

piece of wood to occupy its beak, but on no account should it be allowed to bite anything painted or varnished. Hen Grey Parrots in breeding condition spend a lot of time scratching up the sand at the bottom of the cage, as they would do when excavating a tree trunk hollow. If the litter on the floor is objected to, instead of preventing the poor bird from indulging its natural instinct by the insertion of a ridiculous grating, have a

Pink feathers in Grey Parrots are seen occasionally and arouse the interest of fanciers.

detachable sheet of zinc on each side of the cage of a depth sufficient to catch the flying sand and prevent it from passing through the bars. It is often asked whether or not parrots understand the meaning of what they say. In the majority of cases undoubtedly they do not, but it is almost equally certain that the more intelligent birds do so in some instances. A Grey Parrot is also quick to associate ideas by sight or sound. A hen bird in my possession imitates the blowing of a nose either on being shown a handkerchief or on hearing a sneeze. The pouring out of water

also evokes from her a realistic gurgling noise which says more for her quickness of mind than for the table manners of her former associates. Very young parrots have grey irises but the colour soon changes to the pale yellow eye of the adult. There is not the slighest evidence that Grey Parrots, as is sometimes stated, take nearly twenty years to become sexually mature. In a wild state they almost undoubtedly begin to breed not later than their fourth year and possibly one or even two years sooner.

When newly imported, the species is apt to be delicate and sensitive to cold and may even, from overcrowding and neglect on the voyage, be found to be suffering from parrot fever (psittacosis), an infectious and always fatal complaint. Only complete scorching with a blowtorch will render a cage occupied by a diseased bird safe for a successor. When acclimatized, the Grey Parrot is perfectly hardy in climates similar to England's and can be wintered in an outdoor aviary without heat.

It has been bred both at liberty, in aviaries, and in close confinement but only on rare occasions, not because there is any real difficulty in getting it to go to nest, but because few people give parrots any encouragement to do so and for some unknown reason a cock bird is extraordinarily difficult to get, the enormous majority being hens. A genuine male is usually a very big, rather gaunt-looking fellow, with, according to some authorities, the bare grey patch behind the eye less rounded and more elliptical in shape. If tame, he is generally a brilliant talker, though most hens also talk well, only a very few being unable to learn anything. If a true pair can be obtained, Grey Parrots are really easier to breed than some parakeets, for the cocks retain their fertility with very little wing exercise, and a good hollow log or barrel partly filled with decayed wood makes a satisfactory nursery for the young. A pair, when first introduced are very slow to make friends, but once mated, become savage and aggressive towards humans. If you want a parrot to be a pet, *don't* get it a partner! Single hen birds not infrequently lay and may die egg-bound if their owners do not give them relief by placing them in a very hot room when they show signs of illness.

The Grey Parrot is subject to colour variation. Birds with an abnormal quantity of pink feathers are not uncommon, also

A Grey Parrot at liberty.

African Parrots

partial albinos; pure albinos with red tails occur, and, rarest of all, wholly white specimens and grey birds with white tails. I once had the transient pleasure of owning a red-tailed albino which a dealer transferred to me for a heroic figure. As the bird was very young and was suffering from parrot fever, its mortal remains soon graced a Scottish museum where I hope one day to see them—for I never set eyes on my expensive purchase, being away from home during its brief sojourn!

The Grey Parrot has been trained to stay at liberty. Birds that have been long caged are liable to need coaxing and watching until they regain their skill in flight, as they are apt to gain a lofty tree-top and then find great difficulty in flying down.

Old writers sometimes refer to the Grey Parrot as the Jaco.

Above: *Grey Parrots in a conventional nesting box.* Below: *Grey Parrots in appropriate conditions are relatively easy to breed and accept varied nesting sites.*

Senegal Parrot
Poeocephalus senegalus
Distribution: Gambia.
Adult male: Green. Head dark greyish, paler on the cheeks. Lower breast and abdomen orange-yellow. Flights dusky with a green tinge on the outer webs. Tail short: greenish brown. Bill black. Length nine and one-half inches.
Adult female: Similar but with a much narrower and finer head.

A popular and well-known bird and probably one of the best of the small parrots for anyone who requires a cage pet. The Senegal becomes much attached to one person or to one sex and is lively and playful, learning to say a few words or short sentences. Its chief failings are a slate-pencil screech and a tendency to bite in moments of mischievous excitement, but not all individuals possess this vice.

In Senegal Parrots, the male achieves a length of 9½ inches.

The Senegal is said to have been wintered without heat, but little is known about any of the *Poeocephali* as aviary birds.

The Senegal Parrot usually behaves stupidly at liberty; even tame specimens quickly lose their way and are nervous and clumsy about flying down, dashing swiftly around their owner, only to take perch once more in the top of a high tree.

The food should consist of a seed mixture of two parts canary, two parts millet, one part sunflower and one part peanuts, with plenty of fruit if the bird's digestion remains in good order.

Senegals have laid eggs in captivity, but the cock of the pair killed the hen.

Lovebirds

Nyassa Lovebird
Agapornis lillianae
Distribution: Nyassaland, Northern Rhodesia.
Adult male: Forepart of head orange-red, cheeks and throat slightly paler and merging into pink. Back of head yellow merging into green. Remainder of plumage green, slightly paler on the breast. Bill red. A white circle round the eye. Total length four inches. Size about that of a Budgerigar.
Adult female: Resembles the male. According to some

Lime and elm twigs are the preferred nesting medium of a pair of Nyassa Lovebirds.

authorities has a slightly broader beak.
Immature: Slightly less richly coloured than the adult.

Unknown to aviculture until recent times, this pretty little lovebird has now become one of the commonest of aviary birds in many parts of the world, threatening to rival even the Budgerigar in popularity. It is easily kept in any kind of aviary, birdroom or flight cage. The main occupation of its existence is the rearing of a numerous progeny, clutch after clutch of eggs being laid with only a pause of a few weeks for the moult. The only check on its fertility in captivity lies in the circumstance that the unhatched embryos are somewhat intolerant of a dry environment, while in cold weather a proportion of the hens are subject to egg-binding. Some aviculturists claim to have overcome the former difficulty, when breeding Nyassas under cover, by providing nest boxes with a false bottom filled with sponge or sphagnum moss kept soaking wet, and separated from the mass of twigs and bark composing the actual nest by a piece of wire gauze. One breeder even went so far, with successful results, as to soak the eggs daily in warm water from the tenth day of incubation, relying on the devotion to their eggs characteristic of lovebirds to keep the hen from deserting under the constant interference. Five eggs form the normal clutch, though larger numbers have been recorded. Lime and elm twigs make the best nesting material and the supply must be renewed even after the young are hatched. The cock Nyassa feeds his sitting mate and spends a good deal of time with her in the nest. The difficulty of distinguishing the sexes by their appearance is largely made up for by the facility with which true pairs can be recognized by their behaviour. No self-respecting hen Nyassa dreams of delaying to go to nest

A lutino *Nyassa Lovebird.*

at the earliest possible moment. If after the lapse of a few weeks, no eggs have appeared, you may be sure your birds are cocks, while double clutches of from eight to

In lutino parrot varieties, as in the lutino Nyassa Lovebird, areas normally green become yellow.

ten infertile eggs are equally certain proof that you have nothing but hens.

Nyassa Lovebirds are quite hardy, but their winter treatment in outdoor aviaries presents some difficulty owing to the egg-binding danger already mentioned, coupled with the fact that the removal of the nest logs in which they sleep is apt to be followed by an outbreak of chills. On the whole it is best to move the nests into the aviary shelter during the autumn and heat the shelter, resigning oneself to a proportion of useless clutches until the warm weather returns.

The Nyassa Lovebird is reputed to be fairly quiet in mixed company, although it agrees well with its own kind, I should not care to trust it with valuable Budgerigars or finches, as some individuals can be very savage.

The food should consist of a mixture of two parts canary, two parts millet, one part oats, one part hemp, and one part sunflower. Green food may be offered, but they seldom eat much.

The species interbreeds freely with nearly allied lovebirds; the hybrid with the Black-cheek is rather pretty and perfectly fertile.

Fischer's Lovebird
Agapornis fischeri

Distribution: Uosure, Victoria Nyanza.

Adult male: General plumage green, paler on the breast. A band of bright orange-red across the forehead; the same colour in a paler shade on the cheeks and throat where it merges into rose colour and old-gold. Head and back of neck strongly washed with dull olive green. A patch of dark blue above the root of the tail. Tail feathers green, tipped with blue. Bill bright red. A white circle round the eye. Total length five and one-quarter inches. Somewhat larger than the Nyassa Lovebird.

Adult female: Similar to the male. Often appears larger and of a paler but brighter colour.

Immature: Resembles the adult, save that the olivaceous shade extends much further 'round the sides of the neck and down to the green mantle. Forehead slightly

An artist's rendition of Fischer's Lovebird.

less richly coloured.

This lovebird, formerly to all intents and purposes unknown to aviculture, was in 1926 imported in large numbers and is now a well-known aviary bird over a great part of the world. It seems a hardy and prolific species, some birds received by the writer in early autumn rearing their first brood in the open flight of an unheated aviary in the middle of winter. The weather at the time was exceptionally bad, and when the young birds were nearly ready to fly a raging blizzard covered the roof of the aviary with snow. A bitter hurricane blew for many days, during which it never stopped freezing and later there was a heavy fall of rain.

The nesting habits and requirements of Fischer's Lovebird resemble those of the Nyassa. It agrees fairly well with its own kind, though some pairs will kill their neighbour's young. A simple bird I introduced into an aviary of finches proved exceedingly spiteful, quickly murdering two of its companions.

Hardy as it is in the ordinary way, Fischer's Lovebird will not thrive outdoors in winter if its nesting logs be removed, even though it be driven into the aviary shelter at night. It is necessary, therefore, to allow it to go on breeding and if the hens should get egg-bound to warm the shelter and put the logs inside. If, as is likely, few young are reared in the over-dry atmosphere of the shelter, the logs can be hung in the open flight where the rain will fall on them as soon as the warm nights return. Strange to say, though so difficult to sex when adult, young birds just out of the nest show a decided difference in the size of the head and beak.

Young birds sometimes leave the nest fully fledged, but unable to fly. As no bird is more easily injured by a fall than a young lovebird it is prudent to lay a heap of fine resilient twigs beneath the entrance of the nest. The youngsters, when they emerge, should be picked up and put in a cage with clean blotting paper on the floor. Plenty of well-soaked millet and canary spray millet, crushed soaked hemp, shelled soaked sunflower, and stale

A pair of Fischer's Lovebirds; the female is larger and paler.

brown bread crumbs should be sprinkled on the paper and renewed as they get dry or scratched into corners. Within forty-eight hours the young birds will begin to feed themselves if kept in a warm place. Care must be taken to provide both soaked millet and cracked hemp as some nestlings will starve sooner than begin on millet and vice versa. As soon as the young birds are feeding well, the seed can be put in a dish and sand can replace the paper on the floor of the cage, the size of which should be increased as the occupants learn to use their wings. After a fortnight, dry seed should be substituted for soaked, as they eat the latter so greedily that they may grow over-fat and die of apoplexy. This initial wing weakness in the young is most common when the parents are not fully recovered from the effects of the voyage. If it persists in later broods, tall, mould-filled boxes with no wooden bottoms may be substituted for whatever is in use. The mould should reach to within eighteen inches of the entrance hole and the interior must, of course, be climbable.

Fischer's Lovebirds should be fed on the same diet as Nyassas.

Masked Lovebird
Agapornis personata
Distribution: Tanganyike Territory, Nyassaland.
Adult male: Head blackish or blackish brown merging into the yellow of the neck and upper breast, the latter sometimes tinged with orange on the throat. Remainder of plumage green, paler on the abdomen. Lower rump tinged with dull, dark blue. Tail marked with black. Bill red. Large white circles 'round eye. Total length five and three-quarter inches.

Yellow and blue varieties of the Masked Lovebird.

Adult female: Resembles the male. Often larger.
Immature: Slightly less richly coloured than the adult.

This very striking-looking lovebird has become one of the commonest parrots on the bird market. It is among the hardiest of its tribe and among the readiest to go to nest; but it is also, next to the Peach-face, the most spiteful; although, to do it justice, less addicted to wholly unprovoked aggression than *A. roseicollis*. It will live well in an indoor or outdoor aviary, or in a flight cage, but it is cruel and stupid to confine it, or any other lovebird, in quarters so cramped that it cannot nest or freely use its wings.

The Masked Lovebird needs moisture in the nest for the successful development and hatching of the embryo chicks. For this reason the nest logs or boxes should be hung in the open flight where rain can fall on them. My own hens appear able to lay without trouble even in the coldest weather, but a friend of mine lost a hen from egg-binding, and if this ailment is feared, the only plan is to hang the nest logs in a heated shelter during the cold months and risk poor hatching results until spring returns.

The Masked Lovebird lines its

An incubating Masked Lovebird hen.

nest with fine twigs and strips of bark and continues to add material after the young have hatched, so the nest must be a big one or the young will be cramped. Young birds which leave the nest in winter I catch up and treat as recommended in the article on Fischer's Lovebird.

The Masked Lovebird breeds continually, only stopping for the moult. Four eggs are the normal clutch, and the cock spends a good deal of time in the nest with his mate. The sexes are very hard to distinguish, but if you choose a specimen with a wide skull and one with a narrow one you will probably have a true pair. If you have not, you will soon be enlightened by the bird's behaviour, for hens always go to nest without delay.

As already stated, the Masked Lovebird has a fiery temper, but unlike most pugnacious birds, it is not aroused to evil deeds by prosperity and cowed by disturbance and misfortune, but vice versa. It is exceedingly risky to confine several adult birds in a cage or travelling box, as, exasperated by the discomfort of their cramped quarters, they are likely to emulate the exploits of the Kilkenny cats. I have had a bird torn to bits by its companions on a two hour's journey. On the other hand one aviculturist has found the species tolerably well-behaved in mixed company when not interfered with, and my own two pairs, though they have had a couple of shindies and removed the end of a few toes, have at least refrained from murdering each other's young in a twenty-four foot by eight foot by eight foot aviary. On the whole, however, to prevent accidents and mutilation that spoils the birds for show, I would certainly advise each pair being kept alone.

On first leaving the nest some young birds of the brood— apparently of the same sex—have the upper mandible streaked with black.

The London Zoological Gardens have a very interesting cock which is blue where the normal bird is green, and white where the normal one is yellow; the black head being retained. It is greatly to be hoped that a blue strain may be bred from it.

The Masked Lovebird has the squeaking, chittering cries of its near relations, but is not disagreeably noisy.

It should be fed like the Nyassa Lovebird and is fond of oats softened by soaking. The writer hand-reared a three parts grown nestling on porridge brown bread moistened by chewing in the mouth. The little bird was remarkably nervous, intelligent, wary and alert; and, as one would say of a child, in all respects strangely old for its age. It grew up to be a most cheery and amusing pet. A blue strain has been reported in Europe.

Peach-faced Lovebird
Agapornis roseicollis
Distribution: Southwestern Africa and possibly parts of Southeastern Africa.

Pied Peach-faced Lovebird—in piebaldness, dark coloration is missing from some areas of the plumage.

Adult male: Dull green, paler on the breast. Forehead bright rose-red; cheeks and throat rosy pink with a greyish tinge at the edge of the cheeks. Rump brilliant blue. Tail short; blue-green with black and fiery pink markings. Bill coral-red. Total length six inches: about twice as large as a Budgerigar. *Adult female:* Resembles the male; usually, but not invariably, duller in colour.
Immature: Has green areas of the plumage more brownish olive. Forehead brownish; cheeks and throat brownish pink. Base of bill dark. Adult plumage is assumed within a very few months.

Although, like all members of the lovebird family, the Peach-face is quite unsuited to life in a small cage; it will, if provided with a nest box to breed in and branches to nibble, readily adapt itself to life in any kind of aviary,

Lovebirds

birdroom, or even flight cage. There is, unfortunately, no absolutely certain way of distinguishing the sexes by their plumage. Since, however, the Peach-face belongs to that section of the lovebird family of which the main occupation is the reproduction of its species on every possible occasion, an aviculturist need never remain long in doubt as to whether he possesses a true pair. If the birds are not moulting, are in good condition and do not within a couple of months go to nest, they are males. If they both visit the logs and carry in building material on their backs, they are females. If only one carries building

Peach-faced Lovebirds are naturally active and profit from larger enclosures.

material and the other feeds it, they are all right. Peach-faces will make use of any kind of box or hollow log if it be sufficiently roomy to contain a good supply of fine strips of the bark of twigs of lime, elm, or poplar. Unlike some lovebirds their attempts at breeding are not easily rendered abortive by the fact that the nest is in a dry situation. The hen bird alone sits, but the cock joins her in the nest at night, and may also enter it in times of emergency, especially when the young are very small and danger appears to threaten.

The Peach-face is an exceedingly spiteful bird, which will neither agree with its own kind, nor tolerate neighbours of other species, even those considerably larger than itself. It has also an annoying predilection for biting toes. Sometimes the injury is inflicted in the ordinary course of combat with rivals, but in some cases it becomes an actual vice, parents maiming their young before they are independent and youngsters mutilating each other long before they are old enough to quarrel about mates or nesting places. There is no cure for the bad habit and birds addicted to it are best got rid of.

Some aviculturists have been successful in wintering the Peach-faced Lovebird in outdoor aviaries, but the writer has not found it completely hardy in very severe weather.

The species should be fed on canary, millet, and oats, but hemp and sunflower are liable to produce feather plucking; chickweed and other green food should be supplied to birds rearing young.

In addition to the chittering cries uttered by many members of the family, the Peach-face has

A male Grey-headed Lovebird (Agapornis cana).

a disagreeable penetrating shriek which has earned it a bad name with some aviculturists.

Although not every pair can be trusted to stay, Peach-faces can be bred at liberty during the summer months. Before being released they should be thoroughly accustomed in an aviary to the type of nest box they will find awaiting them in the garden; they do not take at all readily to natural holes in trees. If, as one observer states, the Peach-face in its native land breeds in the nest of the Sociable Weaver-bird, this reluctance is easily explained.

A hand-reared, talking Peach-face has been recorded, who after biting his owner, would say "Naughty Joey!"

Semi-lutinistic specimens have been reported.

Asiatic Parrots

Closely confined, Red-sided Eclectus Parrots seldom survive more than two or three years.

Red-sided Eclectus Parrot
Lorius pectoralis
Habitat: New Guinea and many neighbouring islands, North Queensland.
Adult male: General plumage brilliant green; bastard-wing, primary coverts, primary and secondary quills deep blue. Outer tail feathers deep blue. Under wing-coverts, auxillaries, and a large patch on the side of the body bright red. Upper mandible red with a yellowish tip; eyes brown. Total length fourteen inches. Size somewhat larger than a Blue-fronted Amazon.

Adult female: General plumage bright red, inclining to crimson on the back, wings, and base of the tail. A band of blue across the mantle, a narrow circle of blue 'round the eye; abdomen and sides of the body purplish blue; bastard-wing, primary coverts, outer portions of the primaries and tips of the secondaries deep blue. Tip of tail orange-red. Bill black.

The Eclectus Parrots have long been noted for the striking difference in the plumage of the sexes and some writers have mentioned them as a curious example of species where the female is more richly coloured than the male. Why a crimson bird should be considered more ornate than a brilliant green one is a little hard to understand.

When confined in parrot cages, Eclecti are usually melancholy and apathetic and seldom survive for more than two or three years. Occasionally, however, one meets with individuals—usually females—which have been carefully tamed and petted and allowed a good deal of liberty in the room, with the result that they have become docile and affectionate and have even learned to say a few words.

Of the Eclectus Parrot's voice, only one favourable thing can be said—that he does not make very free use of it. Indeed, if he be at all dispirited and out of sorts he will not utter a sound of any kind. Let him be a little extra lively, however, or slightly alarmed, and the best efforts of an excited Lemon-crest or macaw are as music to the truly awful "Crrah!" he lets off. It goes through you like a knife, and I doubt if the whole realm of nature contains another sound so incredibly harsh.

Eclectus Parrots should be fed like Grey Parrots, fruit being an important item in their diet. They need plenty of warmth when newly imported, but when acclimatized can stand a fair amount of cold. Being exceedingly sensitive to septic fever infection, they must be kept in very clean surroundings. On the whole they do best in an aviary in summer and, if the aviary shelter be not well-warmed, they should be loose in a birdroom during the winter; or if that be not possible, in a large flight cage. When in breeding condition they are of a somewhat savage and uncertain temper, especially with their own species.

Pure Red-sided Eclectus do not appear to have been bred, but hybrids and nearly allied species have been reared in captivity. A hen Eclectus that laid in a cage was given a fowl's egg to sit on, which she hatched successfully. It is not recorded how she got on with her active foster child!

My efforts to induce Eclectus Parrots to stay at liberty were completely unsuccessful. I did not, however, experiment with the male of a breeding pair whose mate was confined in an aviary.

Red-sided Eclectus Parrot—in no other parrot species are male and female so diversely colored.

Blue-fronted Amazons reach a length of 14 to 15 inches.

Blue-fronted Amazon
Amazona aestiva

Distribution: Brazil, Paraguay, Argentina.

Adult male: Green with faint bluish reflections on the fore-neck and breast. Feathers of hind-neck and mantle barred with black. Forehead pale blue; crown, cheeks and throat yellow. Some birds have the crown all blue and others all yellow. Bend of wing yellow mixed with red. Outer web of primaries bluish. Secondaries show a large patch of red; also blue and green colouring. Tail feathers green with terminal portion paler golden-green. A red patch near the base of the outer ones. Bill blackish. Length fourteen to fifteen inches.

Adult female: Resembles the male but has a narrower skull. The bend of the wing is usually red.

Immature: Have the blue and yellow areas of the plumage reduced in size.

The Blue-fronted Amazon is the best known and most commonly imported of all the parrots, the numbers in captivity exceeding those even of the Grey. It takes well to cage life and usually makes an excellent talker and mimic. If not quite equal to the African bird in the number of words it can learn to repeat clearly, it surpasses its rival in its power of giving the general effect of a conversation, a song, or a person in tears; the mimicry being often exceedingly ludicrous. Some years ago my mother had a Pekingese dog of a very irascible disposition who particularly objected to the ministrations of the vet. An Amazon we had at the time learned to give a most realistic representation of a stormy interview between Che Foo and his medical adviser, the infuriated yells of the dog mingling with the soothing words wherewith his friends endeavoured to assuage his ill-humour.

The Blue-fronted Amazon has two failings. Like all its tribe it screams badly in moments of excitement and most, though not all, are liable to give an occasional nip even to their best friends, either when their jealousy is aroused by the presence of another parrot, or simply out of pure mischief. Covering the bird's cage as a punishment will sometimes teach it to control its desire to give vocal expression to its exuberant feelings, while if the bite is not inflicted from fear or active dislike, a gentle cuff, accompanied by a sharp word of reproof, will encourage better manners.

Being very common and easy to obtain, Blue-fronted Amazons suffer badly from the callousness and cupidity of dealers. Disgracefully cramped and over-crowded on the voyage, the poor birds arrive in a filthy condition, often suffering from incurable infectious enteritis, and in any case, in a state of health and plumage which renders them liable to chills on the slightest provocation. The advice given as to the general treatment of caged parrots is applicable to this Amazon. It is probably safe to say that nine-tenths of the Blue-fronted at the present time in captivity in this country are being kept in cages half the proper size, do not see a bath from one year's end to another, and get very little fruit. But lots of unwholesome milk and butter which may lead to tuberculosis, if not to digestive troubles and feather plucking, is given.

The Blue-fronted Amazon should be given a seed mixture of two parts canary, one part millet, one part oats, one part hemp, one part sunflower, and one part peanuts, with plenty of fruit. An Amazon will eat half an apple a day, or a whole one if the fruit be small.

Blue-fronted Amazons have been bred, but only rarely. This is not because the birds are in any way difficult to get into breeding condition, but simply because no one bothers to give proper breeding accommodation to such large and common birds. A hollow tree-trunk makes the best nest, but a box or barrel partly filled with decayed mould will also

serve. The female must not be allowed to lay when the nights are cold. Paired Blue-fronts, like Greys, become excessively savage.

In suitable climates Amazons can be wintered in an outdoor aviary. In adverse climates they sometimes suffer from

An excellent talker and mimic, the Blue-fronted Amazon adapts well to life in a cage.

pneumonia and enteritis. An Amazon attacked by the latter complaint often passes a quantity of blood, but a very high temperature and a diet of bread and scalded milk for two or three days will usually effect a cure.

The Blue-fronted Amazon has been kept with success at liberty, though newly-released birds which have been long caged need watching in case they lose their bearings.

In the writer's collection is living a very beautiful lutino hen Blue-front. The areas which are blue in the ordinary form are in her case white; those which are green are the richest golden yellow; while the red is retained. Her eyes are red, her feet and beak are of a flesh colour. The crimson and white of her secondaries against the golden background of her body plumage are extraordinarily lovely. A

Yellow-fronted Amazon

similar bird is figured in Salvadori's old book on parrots together with another very beautiful lutino Amazon, each of whose yellow feathers is lightly edged with red, producing a scaly appearance. A blue specimen of this parrot is also on record.

Yellow-fronted Amazon
Chrysotis ochrocephala
Distribution: Brazil, Ecuador, Venezuela, Trinidad, Eastern Peru.
Adult: Green, paler on the head and yellower on the breast. Feathers of neck and mantle with dusky edges. Crown yellow. Flights blue and green with

blackish webs. A red bar on the secondaries. A fiery-red patch near the base of the outer tail feathers. Bill blackish with flesh-coloured base. About the size of the Blue-front.
Immature: Appears to lack the yellow on the crown and the red on the wing.

The Yellow-fronted Amazon is not infrequently imported and makes an amusing talker and mimic. Dr. Butler mentions one that had entirely forgotten its own language and expressed all its emotions of rage, pleasure, fear, etc., as a child would, shouting and crying when startled or angry. It also appeared to understand the meaning of some of the sentences it used. If anyone dressed for a walk appeared in the room the parrot would say: "Are you going out?" "Are you going to the park?" "There's a cat in the park." "Good-bye!"

Mr. Brook had a specimen that was almost a pure lutino, showing only a slight trace of green. The female is said to have less yellow on the crown, a paler iris and a narrower beak.

Treatment is as for the Blue-front.

Levaillant's Amazon (often Double Yellow Head)
Amazona oratrix
Distribution: Mexico, Yucatan, and Honduras.
Adult: Green, paler and bluer on the breast. Head and neck golden yellow, paler on the crown. Mantle often flecked with yellow. Shoulder and bend of wing showing pinkish-red and yellow feathers. Wing-bar pinkish red, flights also showing blue, green and black colouring. Tail feathers with pale green tips. Outer pair with a blue edging. A patch of fiery red near the base. Bill whitish. Iris red with inner ring

Levaillant's Amazon

yellow. Total length fifteen inches. Size about that of the Blue-front. *Immature:* Show less yellow and have more green on cheeks and crown.

Levaillant's Amazon or the Double-fronted, as it is often called, is a rather striking-looking parrot with its yellow head, white beak and red eyes. It always gives the impression of being a colour variety rather than the typical representative of a species. It is, perhaps, scarcely as hardy as the Blue-front, needing more room and exercise and the best of feeding with plenty of fruit. Individuals vary greatly in disposition, some being amiable, others fierce or treacherous. Though noisy, Levaillant's Amazon often proves a brilliant talker. Canon Dutton had one which sang seven songs, did the French military exercises, said other things and swore volubly like a French sailor, and was always ready to perform at command. It was a gentle bird and bore its master no malice, though he had to hold it during a painful operation.

An old portrait by Marc Geerarts represents Lady Arabella Stuart with a Levaillant's Amazon, a Red and Green Macaw, and a pair of Red-faced Lovebirds. The date of the picture must be about 1590 and it is interesting to find that these birds were known to English aviculture at so early a date.

The female is said to be smaller and to have a shorter and broader beak.

Levaillant's Amazon can be wintered out-of-doors.

Panama Parrot
Amazona panamensis
Habitat: Panama, Veraguas, Colombia.
Adult: Green with faint bluish reflections on the crown, cheeks, throat and breast. A patch of yellow on the forepart of the crown. A patch of red at the shoulder. Outer webs of primaries dark blue. Secondaries show the usual red patch found in nearly all Amazons. Bill yellowish. Length twelve to fourteen inches.
Immature: Entire head green.

A rare Amazon in captivity.

Yellow-naped Amazon

Treatment as for the Yellow-shouldered.

Yellow-naped Amazon
Amazona auropalliata (often miscalled "Panama Parrot")
Distribution: Western side of Central America.
Adult: Green, paler on the breast and much paler on the head. Feathers of the sides of the neck and upper breast faintly barred with dusky colour. Nape yellow; a few yellow feathers often present on the forehead. Flights green and blue with black inner webs, a pinkish red bar on the secondaries. Tail green with terminal half pale yellowish green.

A patch of fiery red near the base of the outer tail feathers. Bill horn-grey with yellowish base. Total length fourteen inches. About the size of the Blue-front. (The male is often brighter and larger than the female with greater sheen to the feather.)

The Yellow-naped Amazon is a somewhat rare bird in captivity, but very abundant in a wild state. An observer, writing in the year 1896, comments on the large numbers that came to roost in the vicinity of the houses of the town. It is known to make an excellent talker.

The female is said to have a narrower beak, more arched, and with a shorter terminal hook. The

Like the other amazon species, the Yellow-shouldered Amazon cannot be sexed reliably by coloration.

treatment should be that of the Blue-front.

Yellow-shouldered Amazon *Amazona ochroptera,* also *Amazona barbadensis barbadensis*

Distribution: Island of Aruba off Venezuela.

Adult: Green with bright bluish reflections on the lower cheeks and breast. Crown, throat, and feathers below the eye golden yellow, orange-salmon at the base. Forehead frosted with white. Feathers of neck, mantle, and rump barred at the tip with black; the barring being most pronounced on the lower part of the back of the neck. Bend of the wing yellow, or yellow and red. Thighs yellow. Tail feathers green with pale tips, the outer ones showing a patch of wine colour at the base. Flight feathers blue on the outer web, secondaries showing a large patch of red. Bill whitish horn. Iris orange. Total length thirteen to thirteen and one-half inches. Wings about eight and one-half inches. Slightly smaller than the Blue-fronted Amazon.

The Yellow-shouldered Amazon is a rarely imported bird. Like all the species smaller than the Blue-front, and many that are larger, it does much better in a flight cage, birdroom, or aviary than in a parrot cage. The food should be that of the Blue-fronted Amazon.

Old German aviculturists describe this parrot as very easily tamed but showing great individual variation in its powers of mimicry. Sounds were apt to be picked up more easily than words.

The female is said to have the region of the lower mandible, lower breast, and abdomen sky blue, and all the other colours duller.

Mealy Amazon
Amazona farinosa
Distribution: Guianas.
Adult: Green, brighter on the cheeks. Neck, mantle, and rump show a mealy tinge. Feathers of back of crown and back of neck tipped with blackish colour, the latter also showing a bluish lilac tint towards the ends. A spot or patch of yellow, or yellow and

Mealy Amazon

scarlet on the crown. Inner web of primaries black; secondaries show an area of red, dark blue, and green. A little red at the bend of the wing. Tail green at the base; yellowish-green for the terminal half. Bill light horn colour. Length fifteen inches. Larger than the Blue-fronted Amazon.

The Mealy Amazon does somewhat better in an aviary than a cage and can be wintered out-of-doors. Its treatment should be that of the Blue-front.

Canon Dutton had a specimen which was extremely talented, though its songs and conversations were in native dialect; it was also gentle and friendly but unfortunately noisy.

Guatemalan Amazon
Amazona guatemalae
Distribution: Mexico, Guatemala, Honduras.
Adult male: Green with a slight mealy tinge on the mantle and wings. Forepart of crown blue, merging into dull lilac towards the back of the head, and dull olive green tinged with lilac on the neck. From the centre of the crown to the base of the neck the feathers show a dark edging of an increasingly pronounced character. Tail feathers green with the lower half yellowish green. Tips of primaries black. Secondaries show a large area of pinkish red and dark blue. Bill bluish black; iris orange-red. Length about sixteen inches. Somewhat larger than the Blue-fronted Amazon.

A rarely imported bird not likely to differ from the better known Mealy Amazon in its character. The female is said to have a broader beak with a coarser terminal hook.

Guatemalan Amazon

Plain-coloured Amazon
Amazona farinosa inornata
Distribution: Panama, Venezuela, Ecuador, Bolivia.
Adult: Green, brighter on the forehead, cheeks, and breast. Neck and mantle showing a mealy tinge. Feathers of back of crown and back of neck strongly marked with purplish black at the tip. Primaries blackish. Secondaries marked with red and dark blue, as well as green and black. A trace of red at the bend of the wing. Tail feathers green at the base and yellowish green for the

terminal half. Eye large. Bill light horn colour. Length fifteen inches. Larger than the Blue-fronted Amazon.

Not much appears to have been recorded of this big Amazon. A specimen in my collection proved amiable with other parrots and capable of wintering out-of-doors. It had a loud and unmusical voice and some talent for mimicry. It seemed amiable in mixed company.

Artist's rendition of the rare Mercenary Amazon.

Mercenary Amazon
Amazona mercenaria

Distribution: Peru, Ecuador, Bolivia.

Adult male: Green, brighter on the cheeks and paler on the breast. Back of neck and mantle with a mealy tinge. Feathers of crown, neck, and upper mantle tipped with purplish black, the marking being heavy on the neck and faint elsewhere. Primaries with green bases and blackish webs. Secondaries showing a large patch of red, as well as dark blue. Bend of wing shows a few red and yellow feathers. Tail tipped with greenish yellow, outer feathers with a large wine red patch in the middle. Bill dusky, yellowish near the base. Total length thirteen and one-half inches. Size about that of the Blue-front.

Immature: Said to lack the red wing-bar.

I have never seen a living specimen of this Amazon, so I am unable to say whether scientists are justified in ascribing to it a more mercenary nature than other parrots!

It is said to make a good talker in its own country and was exhibited at the Zoological Gardens in England in 1882.

Green-headed Amazon
Amazona virenticeps

Distribution: Costa Rica and Veraguas.

Adult: Green, yellower on the cheeks and breast. Crown of head tinged with blue at the front and lilac at the back, the same lilac tinge persisting at the back of the neck. Feathers of the hind part of the crown and neck edged with blackish colour. Mantle with a mealy tinge. Tail green at the base and yellowish green for the terminal half. A trace of dull orange near the base of the outer feathers. Flight feathers blackish on the webs. Secondaries showing a large patch of red; also dark blue and green. Bill bluish black. Total length about sixteen inches. Larger than the Blue-front.

This big Amazon is rare in captivity: it is really only a local race of the Guatemalan from which it is hardly distinguishable.

Festive Amazon
Amazona festiva
Distribution: Amazon Valley, up to Eastern Peru.
Adult: Green, brighter and sometimes bluer on the cheeks and mealy on the back. A narrow line across the forehead, and feathers between eye and beak wine red. Tips of feathers above and behind the eye blue and a trace of blue on the crown. A trace of dark edging to the feathers of the neck. Upper rump crimson. Bastard wing dark blue. Outer edge of primaries dark blue. Secondaries green with a tinge of dark blue. Tail green. Outer feathers with the merest trace of wine red near the base of the quill. Bill dusky. Total length fourteen and one-half inches. Size about that of the Blue-front.

The Festive Amazon is a handsome parrot and has the reputation of being much less noisy than most of its allies. Individuals vary greatly in docility and talent, but the best are said to be brilliant talkers with very clear pronunciation.

Canon Dutton had a yellow specimen for a short time, but it does not seem certain that it was a pure lutino. The natives of South America are credited with producing yellow feathers on green parrots by rubbing them with the poisonous secretion from the skin of a certain frog. Birds without the red eye and pale feet of the true lutino must therefore

be viewed with some suspicion.

The female is said to have a shorter and fuller beak and to be smaller than the male.

The treatment should be that of the Blue-front.

The Festive Amazon, known for its clear pronunciation.

Green-cheeked Amazon (often, Mexican Red Head)
Amazona viridigena
Distribution: Eastern Mexico.
Adult male: Green, very bright on the cheeks and paler on the breast. Cap and feathers in front of eye crimson. A strip of blue or lilac feathers extends over the area behind the eye. Feathers of hind-neck tipped with black. Primaries blue-black with faint pale tips. Secondaries with a

large patch of red; also blue and green. Bill yellowish white, less short and curved than that of the Blue-fronted Amazon. Total length thirteen inches. Size about that of the Blue-front.

Immature: Said to have only the forehead and lores red, the crown being green.

The Green-cheeked is one of the most beautiful of the medium-sized Amazons. It does well in captivity but is somewhat rare and there appears to be little recorded of its character and habits. It should be fed like the Blue-fronted Amazon.

The female is said to have less red on the crown and a smaller beak.

The Green-cheeked Amazon is native to eastern Mexico.

Spectacled Amazon

Spectacled Amazon
Amazona albifrons

Distribution: Western Mexico, Yucatan, Guatemala, Nicaragua, and Costa Rica.

Adult: Green, brighter on the cheeks and breast and faintly barred with black on the neck. Forepart of crown white; rear part blue. Feathers round the eye and between eye and beak, red. Some bright red on the lower edge of the wing. Flight feathers rich dark blue and green with blackish inner webs. A patch of wine red near the base of the outer tail feathers. Bill light yellow. Total length ten and one-half inches. Much smaller than the Blue-front. (Female has less white on the crown, and is smaller and duller than the male.)

Immature: Has less red on the wing, and probably less white and more blue on the crown.

This very small and rather striking-looking Amazon is extremely rare in captivity. It does badly in a parrot cage, but will live well in a flight cage, birdroom, or aviary. Little is known of its ability to stand cold and it would be unwise to expose it to a low temperature without great caution. The few birds the writer has known have been unfriendly and inclined to bite. The food should be that of the Blue-fronted Amazon, without hemp.

Finsch's Amazon
Amazona finschi (also called lilac-crowned parrot)

Distribution: Western Mexico.
Adult male: Green, paler and brighter on the cheeks. Forehead and area between eye and beak dull red. Crown and outer edge of cheeks lilac with a few green feathers interspersed. Feathers of neck and breast edged with black. A pinkish red bar on the wing, flights also showing blue and green areas. Outer tail feathers with paler tips and a yellowish patch on the inner webs. Bill dirty white. Total length thirteen inches. A little smaller than the Blue-front.

In a wild state this parrot is said to fly in large flocks and to be very active and graceful on the wing.

It is uncommon in captivity.

The female is said to have a broader and shorter beak, and is smaller and duller than the male.

Jamaica Amazon

Jamaica, All-green, or Active Amazon
Amazona agilis

Distribution: Jamaica.
Adult: Green, darker on the crown and paler on the breast. A scarlet patch on the lower edge of the wing. Flights blue and green, with black inner webs. Bill greyish-black. Total length ten and one-half inches. Much smaller than the Blue-front.
Immature: Has no red in the wing, and the flights are a duller blue.

Although uncommon in captivity, Finsch's Amazon is pictured here in an aviary.

A very rare parrot which has been exhibited at the Zoological Gardens in England. Unless bred in captivity it will become extinct.

The female is said to have a shorter and broader beak with a shorter terminal hook.

Red-throated or Jamaican Amazon
Amazona collaria

Distribution: Jamaica.

Adult: Green, very bright on the breast and yellowish on the tail coverts. Forehead white; more rarely pink. Crown dark bluish with black edgings to the feathers. Feathers of the neck edged with black and a trace of the same marking on the mantle. Throat deep pink. Outer web of flight feathers slate blue. Tail yellowish green, outer feathers with a deep pink patch near the base. Bill whitish. Length about twelve inches. Smaller than the Blue-front.

The Red-throated is also known as the Jamaican, or the Yellow-billed Amazon.

The Jamaican or Red-throated Amazon is rare in captivity. It has the reputation of being affectionate, but noisy and a poor talker. Like most of the smaller Amazons it needs more exercise than permanent confinement in a parrot cage permits. It should be fed like the Blue-front.

Yellow-lored Amazon
Chrysotis xantholora

Distribution: Yucatan, Cozumel Island, British Honduras.

Adult: Dark green, paler and yellower on the tail-coverts. Feathers edged with black most heavily on the neck, mantle, and upper breast. Forepart of crown white with rear edge dark blue. Feathers above, below, and at the back of eye bright red. Feathers between beak and eye and a small spot under the lower mandible yellow. Flights green and dark blue with blackish inner webs. A patch of scarlet on the lower edge of the wing. A patch of wine red near the base of the outer tail feathers. Bill yellow. Total length ten and one-half inches. Much smaller than the Blue-fronted Amazon.

Immature: Appears to have the crown mainly blue and less red 'round the eye and on the wing.

This curious little Amazon is extremely rare in captivity. It is really a local race of the Spectacled Amazon and should be treated in the same way. It requires more care than its larger relatives.

Yellow-lored Amazon

White-fronted or Cuban Amazon
Amazona leucocephala

Distribution: Cuba, Island of Pines.

Adult: Green, yellowish on the tail coverts. Forehead white, sometimes tinged with rose. Cheeks and an irregular patch on the throat rose red or rose pink.

White-fronted Amazon

Feathers of the forepart of the body edged with black, the marking being heaviest on the head and neck. Feathers of abdomen show a considerable amount of wine colour. Outer web of flights slate blue. Tail yellowish green, outer feathers with a large red or wine red patch near the base. Bill whitish. Total length twelve to thirteen inches. Slightly smaller than the Blue-front.

The Cuban is the most frequently imported of the group of dark green Amazons with pink or white on the face and throat. It is a very beautiful bird but is noisy and an indifferent talker and does better in an aviary, birdroom, or

From left to right: *Red Lored Parrot, two Orange Winged Parrots, Blue-fronted Parrot and Mealy Amazon.*

flight cage than in very close confinement.

Newly imported Cubans sometimes suffer from infectious maladies contracted while they are overcrowded on the voyage. I remember a lot of twenty birds which seemed in the best of health for two or three weeks after arrival and then began to drop off until not a single one was left.

This Amazon is not a particularly reliable stayer at liberty, but I once had a female which spent the winter free in the garden and paired with a young cock Adelaide Parakeet. Strange to say the latter was bred at liberty and had never known confinement and it is extraordinary that when less than twelve months old he should have deserted the company of his own kind for that of the parrot. When spring came 'round the Adelaide was most attentive in feeding his strange partner and the pair set up house in a hollow oak, but just when the breeding of remarkable hybrids seemed possible the Amazon unfortunately died.

A hybrid Cuban X Blue-fronted Amazon has been bred on the Continent.

Conures

Red-masked Conure
Aratinga rubrolarvata

Distribution: West Ecuador.
Adult: Green. Crown and face red. Some spots of red on the neck. Shoulders, under wing-coverts, thighs, and bend of wing red. Bill yellowish white. Length thirteen and one-half inches.
Immature: Much less red.

The Red-headed Conure is a typical member of a large group of South American parakeets which have a strong family resemblance in character and habits. They make affectionate, intelligent, and playful pets, but are too active to be suited to

The Red-headed Conure is also known as the Red-masked Conure (A. erythrogenys).

permanent confinement in a parrot cage, and if caged must be let out daily for exercise in spite of their fondness for chewing up wood and other relatively soft substances. Most species are hardy and can be wintered in outdoor aviaries. The chief fault of the genus is their excessive noisiness and spitefulness towards parakeets of other families. Like lorikeets they are a little less intolerant of their own kind and also of non-psittacine birds.

They nest fairly freely in captivity and are usually double brooded. In their domestic arrangements they closely resemble lorikeets, and they will use a hollow log or tree trunk in aviary shelter or flight.

They appreciate logs to roost in, but a careful watch must be kept in case a hen tries to lay in cold weather and gets egg-bound. Where this danger has arisen the log must be put in a heated shelter and the birds driven in at night. It may be added that it is a great mistake to leave nests in the aviary out of the breeding season where species are kept which do *not* use them as dormitories. Conures should be fed on a seed mixture of two parts canary, one part millet, one part oats, and one part peanuts with plenty of fruit. Hemp is liable to cause liver disease and feather plucking. The sexes are always much alike.

The Red-headed Conure makes a fair talker.

Mexican Conure
Aratinga holochlora

Distribution: Mexico and Guatemala.
Adult: Green; paler and yellower on the breast. Sometimes a fleck of red on the cheeks. Bill yellowish flesh-colour. Length twelve and one-half inches.

A rarely imported species of no great beauty.

Green Conure
Aratinga leucophthalma

Distribution: Guiana, Trinidad, Colombia, Peru, Bolivia, Brazil.
Adult male: Green. Sometimes with speck of red on the head or neck, or a tinge of wine red on the breast. Bend of wing and under wing-coverts orange-red, the latter merging into yellow. Bill yellowish flesh-colour. Naked skin 'round eye, ashy flesh-colour. Length thirteen and one-half inches.
Immature: Bend of wing yellowish.

A rarely imported species, which, like other large conures, atones for its harsh voice and not particularly beautiful plumage, by unusual intelligence and docility and talent for talking.

The female is said to have a broader beak.

Queen of Bavaria's Conure
Aratinga guarouba

Distribution: Para, Northeast Brazil.
Adult male: General plumage rich golden yellow; flight feathers dark green. Bill pinkish horn; feet flesh-colour. Total length fourteen inches. Size about that of a woodpigeon.
Adult female: Similar to the male but smaller and with a less massive head and beak.
Immature: Nestling plumage shows more green. At a certain stage has cheeks and upper wing-coverts with scattered green feathers.

The Queen of Bavaria's Conure has long been famous for its great rarity; its docility when tamed, and its marvellous golden plumage. I have never been what the late Mr. Jamrach used to call "a strong buyer of conures," but

In the Green Conure, the female reaches a length of 13½ inches.

the Queen of Bavaria was, when it arrived, a welcome addition to my collection. Certainly though not graceful in form, and endowed with a voice as disagreeable as that of any of his noisy congeners, *Conurus guarouba* has a barbaric splendour that cannot fail to attract. He *looks* South American! Although my Queen of Bavarias are not tame, I can well believe that the accounts of their good qualities as pets are not over-rated, for they are continually caressing each other, and play together in the most amusing fashion, shoving and mauling like puppies, yet never evoking a protest by too hard a nip. They are typical conures in all their habits, ruffling their feathers, doing all kinds of gymnastics, and assaulting any parakeet of another family that approaches them, for although single birds are harmless enough in mixed company, pairs are decidedly aggressive.

When newly imported this conure requires warmth and care; afterwards it becomes tolerably hardy, though my birds make a good deal of use of their warmed shelter during cold weather.

Unfortunately, no parakeet in existence is more addicted to the vice of feather plucking. Even the plainest diet combined with plenty of exercise in a large outdoor aviary and a companion of the opposite sex will not prevent some birds from disfiguring themselves.

The Queen of Bavaria's Conure should be fed on sunflower and canary seed with an unlimited supply of apple and other fruit.

When tamed, the species is said to make a good talker, and my hen bird mimics the Barabands with which she lives.

The Queen of Bavaria's Conure is also known as the Golden Conure.

Golden-crowned Conure
Eupsittula aurea
Distribution: Guiana, Amazons, Bolivia, Paraguay.
Adult: Green: forepart of crown and feathers 'round the eye orange-salmon. Rear of crown bluish. Throat, cheeks, and upper breast olive, the cheeks with a faint bluish tinge. Lower breast pale yellowish green. Flights blue-green. Tail tip tinged with blue. Bill blackish. Total length ten and three-quarter inches.

The Golden-crowned Conure has been bred several times on the Continent, but in England only hybrids with the Jendaya appear to have been reared. The species is easily tamed and becomes docile and affectionate, but breeding pairs are spiteful with other birds.

The Golden-crowned Conure can be wintered out-of-doors.

The female is said to have a shorter and broader beak.

Lesser Patagonian Conure
Cyanolyseus patagonus
Distribution: La Plata and

Patagonia.

Adult: Dark, brownish olive, paler and more bronze on the wing, and less olive on the upper breast. A little whitish colour on the upper breast. Abdomen yellow with a large orange-red patch on the centre. Rump pale golden-bronze. Flights slate colour. Bill horn black. Length seventeen and one-half inches.

The Patagonian Conure, though not a gaudy bird, is decidedly handsome in its unusual garb of brown and yellow. Like other big conures it is very intelligent, a good talker and mimic, and an

of other conures.

The female is said to be smaller, with a smaller, shorter and broader back.

Petz' Conure (occasionally, Half Moon)
Eupsittula canicularis

Distribution: Mexico and Central America.

Adult: Glittering olive green. Abdomen bright yellow-green. Throat and upper breast pale yellowish olive brown. Forepart of crown salmon colour. Rear of crown slate blue. Flights blue-green. Bill fleshy-white. Length

Artist's rendition of the Lesser Patagonian Conure.

nine and one-half inches.

Immature: Much less salmon on the forehead.

This little conure is not very often imported, but is said to make a nice pet.

In a wild state it feeds largely on the fruit of the tree Pileus conica and, strange to relate, soils its plumage badly with the sticky juice. This circumstance is not a little remarkable when one recollects how strongly healthy birds object, as a rule, to dirt on

amusing and playful companion. It is recorded of one that he was quiet and well-behaved in respectable company, but raised a great uproar on the appearance of tramps.

The species is quite indifferent to cold, and, it breeds in colonies in burrows in the face of cliffs, is probably tolerant of the presence

Top: *Cuban Conure.*
Bottom: *Finsch's Conure.*

their feathers; but I have seen skins of wild Amazon parrots badly disfigured from the same cause.

It is said that Petz' Conure is difficult to distinguish from the fruit on which it feasts so greedily and is apparently aware of the protective resemblance, as it remains quiet and motionless when a hawk surprises it on a "Parrot fruit" tree, but takes to noisy flight if approached by its enemy elsewhere.

Aztec Conure
Eupsittula astec
Distribution: Southern Mexico, Guatemala, Honduras, Nicaragua, and Costa Rica.
Adult: Green. Throat and upper breast brown. Lower breast yellowish olive brown. Flights tinged with bluish slate. Bill brown horn colour. Length nine and one-half inches.

The Aztec Conure is not very often imported. It has been bred in a flight cage in Jamaica. As with most small conures, more than one brood is produced in a year. The normal clutch consists of four or five eggs.

The female is said to have a broader beak.

Cuban Conure
Eupsittula euops
Distribution: Cuba.
Adult male: Green: cheeks, crown and bend of wing flecked with scarlet. Under wing-coverts scarlet. Bill whitish flesh-colour. Length ten and one-half inches.

A rarely-imported bird, said to be intelligent and amusing.

Brown-eared Conure
Eupsittula ocularis
Distribution: Veraguas and Panama.
Adult: Green, paler and yellower on the breast. Crown slightly

The Cactus Conure should be fed a diet of fruit, seeds, berries and nuts.

been wintered out-of-doors. It has the family failing of noisiness, but is said to agree fairly well with other members of the genus. It becomes very tame and amusing, single birds, and even pairs, showing a lively interest in their owner, running to meet him fluttering and jabbering in a sort of ectasy. The species has been bred in captivity. Treatment as for other conures.

The female is said to be smaller and to have a shorter beak.

Jendaya Conure
Eupsittula jendaya
Distribution: Brazil.

tinged with bluish slate colour. Cheeks, throat and upper breast brown. Some orange feathers below the eye and sometimes a slight tinge of orange on the abdomen. Bill horn-brown. Length nine and three-quarter inches.

The Brown-eared Conure was bred in captivity and found to be quiet with non-psittacine birds and not destructive to shrubs. If teased, the pair performed very quaint antics, but did not bite. Nesting operations lasted nine weeks.

Cactus Conure
Eupsittula cactorum
Distribution: Southeastern Brazil.
Adult: Green. Head tinged with brown and faint slate colour. Flights and tip of tail tinged with slate blue. Throat and upper breast brown. Lower breast yellowish buff. Bill whitish. Length ten and one-quarter inches.
Immature: Crown plain green. Throat and breast olive.

This rather pretty little conure does well in confinement and has

The Jendaya Conure.

The Black-headed (or Nanday) Conure is native to Paraguay.

lower rump green. Mantle and wings green: lower edge of wing and flights partly blue. Tail bronze-green at the base, dark blue at the tip. Bill dusky horn colour. Length twelve inches.

The Jendaya, or Yellow-headed Conure, is a freely imported species which does well in an aviary and is reputed to be peaceable with other birds. It has been bred in England, nesting operations taking about three months from start to finish. The species has some talent for mimicry, but the usual conure failing of a harsh voice and a mischievous beak.

Black-headed or Nanday Conure
Nandayus nanday
Distribution: Paraguay.
Adult: Bright green. Crown brownish black merging into chestnut at the rear edge. Front of cheeks marked with black or

Adult: Head and neck orange-yellow. Breast and under wing-coverts orange-red tinged with olive. Thighs olive and tinged with rust red. Upper rump orange-red;

Closely related to the conures, these Thick-billed Parakeet should be kept and fed the same as conures.

black and chestnut. A pale bluish tinge on the upper breast. Thighs rust red. Flights lower edge of wing and tail blue and green. Bill horn-brown. Length twelve inches. Female with a smaller head and more sharply curved beak.
Immature: Duller.

This rather handsome conure is well-known in confinement and has bred on several occasions. It is noisy, but can be wintered out-of-doors and is said to agree fairly well with other members of the genus. Food and treatment as for other conures.

Thick-billed Parakeet
Rhynocopsitta pachyrhyncha
Distribution: Mexico.
Adult: Green, brighter on the cheeks. Forepart of crown, feathers above and behind eye, shoulders, and a touch on the thighs and lower edge of the wing, red. Lower part of under-coverts yellow. Bill black. Length seventeen inches.
Immature: Less red; bill horn-whitish.

This large conure-like parakeet is extremely rare in captivity. The reason may perhaps be found in the answer of a Mexican trapper to a question put by an American friend of mine as to why he did not catch Thick-bills. "Señor, they no good. Bite like hell. Perhaps catch three, four pair; no can use hands for weeks. Lady no buy; gentleman no buy; and damn bird no good to eat. What de hell de use?"

Nevertheless, according to Karl Plath, the species has some virtues to offset its harsh voice and powerful beak, a tame bird in his collection showing great affection for his little son and following him about with a queer shuffling gait, shaking its tail from side to side.

The Quaker (or Grey-breasted) Parakeet is the only parrot species to build a nest, rather than find or excavate a cavity.

The species would no doubt thrive on the treatment of a conure.

Quaker or Grey-breasted Parakeet
Myopsittacus monachus
Distribution: Bolivia, Paraguay, Argentine, Uruguay.
Adult male: Green, brighter on the rump and belly. Forehead and lower part of cheeks grey with pale edges to the feathers; lower breast greyish olive. Flights and bastard-wing bluish. Tail long and narrow, green slightly tinged with blue. Bill reddish white. Total length eleven and one-half inches. Size about that of a Ringneck.
Adult female: Said to be more bulky and with a much longer and more powerful beak. (Did the

observer mistake the cock for the hen?)

The Quaker Parakeet has the distinction of being the only parrot which is known to build an actual nest. It is an excessively hardy bird and the only thing that will kill it is permanent confinement in a parrot cage. It is highly gregarious in a wild state, even during the breeding season, and the old nests are repaired and re-occupied until they reach a great size. When not employed for the rearing of a brood they are kept in good condition for a dormitory. A species of Teal, *B. monachus*, often lays its eggs in the Quakers' nests and appears to live on quite good terms with

The Crimson-bellied Conure (Pyrrhura rhodogaster) *is known for its constant chatter.*

the rightful owners. The nest itself is entirely composed of sticks and consists of two chambers, an inner and an outer one. As the young brood increase in size the parents sometimes reconstruct and enlarge the nursery. From four to six eggs are usually laid and the period of incubation is thirty-one days.

The Quaker is a noisy bird, continually uttering its "Quak, Quaki, quak-wi, quak-wi, quak-wi, quarr! guarr! quarr!" Some people find its vocal efforts distressing, but in justice it must be admitted that while the Quaker talks far, far too much, he just fails to reach the unendurable pitch in all his remarks. Pet birds are intelligent and amusing. An aviculturist had one which was an excellent talker, its longest sentence being "Merrily danced the Quaker's wife with all her bairns about her." It would do tricks to order. At the command "Act daft!" it would ruffle its feathers, put up one leg, open its beak, and nod its head. At the command "Act proud!" it would turn its beak against its breast and draw up its head. It showed great affection for its owners, but would attack visitors and strange dogs and cats and pull off the maids' caps. It was never shut up in the daytime. It bathed freely and was so indifferent to cold that it would dry itself on the crack between two window sashes through which a keen northeaster was blowing.

The Quaker will flourish in an outdoor aviary and care nothing for the cold. It requires netting of cockatoo strength to confine it, as it can bite through ordinary wire.

For breeding, a large heap of twigs and sticks must be provided and a framework or platform as a foundation for the nest. Both sexes share in the work of building. The Quaker agrees well with its own kind but is very savage with all other birds, a pair delivering a joint attack after the manner of lorikeets.

The Quaker should be fed on canary, millet, oats, and sunflower with peanuts and plenty of fruit. The species has bred at liberty both in England and on the Continent, a pair in Saxony producing a flock of forty birds.

Two of the subspecies of the Brown-throated Conure.

Brown-throated Conure (often Chocolate-face)
Eupsittula pertinax aeruginosa
Ditribution: Colombia, Venezuela, Brazil.
Adult: Green; crown with a slate bluish tinge. Cheeks, throat, and upper breast brown, sometimes some orange feathers 'round the eye. Flights tinged with slate blue. Lower breast yellowish green tinged with more or less orange. Bill whitish. Length ten and one-quarter inches.
Immature: Said to have a greener

Notwithstanding these successes, it cannot be considered an ideal liberty subject. The great majority stay only for a time and then wander away after a few months or even a year. They are also fearfully destructive in the garden, sheering off innumerable branches and committing havoc in the orchard. They are fond of feeding on the araucaria, or monkey-puzzle tree, eating the base of the leaves as we eat the base of the sepals of an artichoke.

crown and an olive throat and breast.

The Brown-throated Conure is freely imported and is an amusing, if noisy, little bird. Single specimens become very tame and playful and can be taught to talk.

The species was bred by Mrs. Williams, who describes the young as having a whitish ring 'round the eye.

Birds in the writer's collection needed artificial heat in winter.

The female is said to have a longer and more slender beak.

Cockatoos and Cockatiel

Palm or Great Black Cockatoo
Microglossus aterrimus
Distribution: Papuan Islands and North Australia.
Distribution: Black, the races from the New Guinea region with a slate grey tinge. A patch of naked pink skin at the base of the beak. Bill of great size and black in colour. Upper mandible notched. Eye large and dark. A long crest of hair-like feathers. Total length twenty-nine inches.

The cheek patches of the Palm Cockatoo turn a more noticeable red when the bird is excited.

Adult female: Smaller and more slender, with a much smaller head and beak.

This extraordinary-looking cockatoo was rare in aviculture until recent years, when a number—mostly males—were imported, both the New Guinea race and the smaller subspecies being represented.

In a wild state the Palm Cockatoo is said to subsist on nuts and on the green centre of the palm cabbage. Its eggs are laid in a hollow tree on a bed of green twigs.

In captivity it has the reputation, when tamed, of being a very gentle bird, not biting even when annoyed, but merely scratching with the tip of its upper mandible. Unlike the *Caltyptorhynci*, it is said to enjoy being petted and there are records of specimens which said a word or two in a very small voice. The curious bare pink skin on the face is capable of changing colour and becomes bluish when the bird is cold or ill.

The Palm Cockatoo's natural calls consist of whistles, screams, and croaks, and when hurt or terrified it utters a loud grating screech.

Palm Cockatoos should be fed on hemp, sunflower, peanuts, and any other nuts or grain that they fancy. They will sometimes also eat apple and green food and milk-sop should be offered to birds with young.

The courtship of the Palm Cockatoo is the quaintest and most ludicrous of any member of the parrot family and perhaps of any bird in the world. Blushing bright red with excitement, the male erects his weird crest, spreads his wings, stamps with his feet, and utters the most incredible assortment of whoops, shrieks and strange clicking noises. At frequent intervals he ducks his head sharply and turning it on one side gazes up adoringly into the face of his beloved.

Male Palm Cockatoos resemble Banksians in that they feed their mates but do not caress them and take no part in the incubation of the eggs. A large natural tree trunk makes the best nest and the birds should be plentifully supplied with leafy branches as they are said to line their nests profusely, no doubt as a precaution against their being filled by tropical rain.

When acclimatized, this species can stand a fair amount of cold.

The Banksian Cockatoo, also known as the Red-tailed Cockatoo.

Banksian Cockatoo
Calyptorhyncus banksii
Distribution: Australia.
Adult male: Black with a dull gloss on the wings and a faint greyish tinge on the breast. A long scarlet bar across the outer tail feathers. Bill greyish black. Length twenty-seven inches.
Adult female: Black, feathers of head, neck, and mantle with dull, pale yellow spots. Breast barred with dull, pale yellow. Under tail-coverts pale yellow and orange-red with black bars and freckling. Tip of tail black: basal portion pale yellow merging into orange-red, with transverse black bars and black freckling.
Immature: In first plumage much resembles the female. With the first moult young males become less spotted and show more red on the tail than females of the same age. With the second moult they become entirely black with scarlet tail bars freckled with black. With the third, adult plumage is assumed in the fourth year.

The Banksian Cockatoo is a variable species of which three or four races exist, differing considerably in size and to some extent in the plumage of the females and the dimensions of the beak.

The typical *C. banksii* is a big race. The female has the head well-spotted and the breast well-barred, the tail feathers showing pale yellow and orange-red colour. The voice of the male when in flight is deep, melancholy, and sonorous.

The Great-billed Banksian Cockatoo is about as large as the typical form and has a larger beak, while the female has scarcely any orange-red in her tail, pale yellow colouring predominating. The Western Black Cockatoo *C. stellatus* is about a third smaller than the two forms already mentioned. The voice of the male is pitched in a higher key and the female is very profusely spotted and barred, her tail being like that of a female *C. banksii* in colouring. This race, of recent years, has been the most frequently imported of the three.

In my collection at the present

Goffin's Cockatoo (Cacatua goffini) is white with a pink tinge on its crest feathers.

time I have a female Banksian Cockatoo which is no larger than a *C. stellatus*, but has hardly any spotting on the head or barring on the breast, while her crest is less rounded than that of a typical Western bird.

In a wild state the Banksian Cockatoo occurs in fairly large flocks, although it seems to be diminishing under persecution for its feathers and flesh, as well as with the settlement of the country. A party of Banksians have a habit, not uncommon among parrots, of refusing to leave a wounded companion, their concern exposing them to still further casualties from a person armed with a gun.

In their nesting habits they resemble the broadtailed parakeets, and differ from most other cockatoos, the cock feeding his sitting mate, but making no attempt to incubate the eggs. The normal clutch consists of two, but single eggs are common.

Banksian Cockatoos are seldom seen in captivity and command very high prices. Presumably the nests are inaccessible and the young troublesome to rear, while adults usually refuse food and die when deprived of their liberty. Birds well on seed are, however, as easy to keep as their commoner white brethren and will survive for a long period either in cage or aviary. A female in my collection must have been at least twenty years in captivity and is still a magnificent specimen showing not a sign of age.

By reason of their great size, their powerful beaks, and their loud and strident cries, Banksians are certainly not everybody's birds, but they have a dignity and charm about them which endears them to the aviculturist who has proper accommodation to place at their disposal. The males become exceedingly tame; so tame, in fact, that it is almost impossible to find one that is of any use for breeding; their affections and interest become so centered in humanity that they have no time for the females of their own kind. No animal will give his master a more disinterested devotion than a Banksian Cockatoo. Unlike most cockatoos they dislike being touched and having their heads scratched, and at most tolerate rather than enjoy such familiarities; they have also little fondness for tit-bits. All that they ask is to be with their master or mistress, and a few kind words and a little flattery will evoke from them a transport of excitement and delight. They throw up their crests into the shape of a Roman helmet, spread their tails and go off into their peculiar love-song, "Kooi, kooi, kooi, kooi." A very tame male who lived for, alas! but a short two years in my collection, was one of the most interesting and delightful birds I have ever kept. With some little difficulty I trained him to fly at liberty and a wonderful sight he was in the air. We have no English bird which in the least resembles *C. banksii* when in flight. The wings and tail of a Black Cockatoo are of great length and give a strangely aeroplane-like appearance. Indeed, my birds used to get wildly excited at the spectacle of an aeroplane in the sky, apparently taking it for a rather odd-looking member of their own species! The flight, though not rapid, is extraordinarily buoyant, the bird having the appearance of a great leaf wafted about by gusts of air. All the time it is on the wing it keeps uttering its strange cry, which in the case of a cock of the large races is wild and melancholy as that of a lost soul. The call of females is harsher and more strident. At first my cock "Teddy" gave us some little trouble. Like many big parrots that have been long confined he was afraid to fly *down* from a height; also, if people went indoors, he was inclined to become anxious and restless and opening his great wings would betake himself to the nearest inn and wait there until his friends came to fetch him home! He was amiable with everyone and ready to perch on an arm or shoulder; or, if such close company were not desired, to sit quietly by you without making himself a nuisance. His particular chum was one of the gardeners. To this man he became so much attached that he would follow his bicycle as he rode home in the evening to the town three miles away and, having seen him safely to his house, he would return long after dusk had fallen. I have often, on a summer evening, sat on the top of the hill near my old home when flocks of wild fowl were

*Glossy Cockatoo
(Calyptorhynchus lathami)*

Lesser Sulphur-crested Cockatoo is white with a lemon yellow crest, and yellow patches on cheeks.

feeding on the grass below. Then faint and far away I would hear Teddy's approaching voice, followed by a roar of wings as company after company of ducks fled in unnecessary consternation and a great dark shadow would drift over my head on noiseless wings as Teddy betook himself to his accustomed perch on the ledge of the stable window. That the ducks should be frightened by Teddy was, perhaps, not unnatural; but strange to say his appearance in the air at first filled my Australian parakeets with as much consternation as if he had been an eagle. As a matter of fact with other birds he was the gentlest and most timid thing imaginable, giving way before the smallest parakeet that approached him closely.

Teddy had a peculiar habit of flying on moonlight nights, and I would often hear him on the wing

at house when one would expect only an Owl Parrot to be active.

Poor fellow! He was one of the first Banksians I ever had and I did not know that, while they can stand dry cold and rain, cold fog and snow are most injurious. I allowed him to roost out one foggy night in late October and he caught a chill, only a very slight chill it seemed, but he just would not feed. I put him in a room at about seventy degrees Fahrenheit (had it been eighty-five degrees I should probably have saved him) but it was no good. Day after day he grew slowly weaker and at length after nearly a fortnight of complete fasting I lost what was in many ways the nicest bird I ever kept.

Banksian Cockatoos should be fed on hemp, sunflower, and peanuts, with a few Brazil nuts. They seldom touch fruit or green food, but occasionally when in an aviary eat a little grass or oats softened in the rain and about to sprout. In a wild state they live largely on grubs, but in captivity they reject mealworms, gentles, and wasp larvae and the larvae of wood-boring beetles. They are, however, exceedingly fond of the little white grubs found inside oak apples and a few will eat smooth caterpillars from rose and apple trees. In collecting oak apples for Banksians look carefully to see that there is no little round hole in the gall, as this means that the insect has made its exit and the "apple" is empty. Banksians are very conservative in their diet and if accustomed to a particular kind of seed will sometimes starve

Leadbeater's Cockatoo is white with pink cheeks. Its long crest is red at base, then yellow, then red, with the tips white.

sooner than touch an unfamiliar one. They are also very sensitive birds and even a tame one will refuse food for some days after arriving at a strange place. As, however, their powers of fasting are considerable no undue anxiety need be felt. A timid bird, which seems very nervous and unhappy, can sometimes be induced to start feeding if turned into an aviary with a companion already used to the place. Banksian Cockatoos are difficult birds to mate up; for not only will the cocks persist in getting too tame and reserving all their affection for human beings; but the hens, unless actually in breeding condition, are snappy and discouraging to their potential suitors. It is only when

Cockatoos and Cockatiel

two birds have been flying together for many months that a good understanding may be hoped for when the hen comes into breeding condition. If the cock is master and bullies his companion, the outlook is hopeless and he can only be tried with a more determined lady who keeps him in his place. Although not great fighters, Banksians do not agree well with their own kind. The hens are jealous of others of their sex and the cocks, especially

The male Gang-gang Cockatoo is known for its brilliant red face and curly feathered crest.

bullied them so badly that I had to remove him.

Banksians may nest at any time of year but the majority lay in autumn and winter. They will use a large, hollow, mould-filled tree trunk and sometimes a barrel. One hen I had insisted on sitting on the ground in a corner of the aviary, like a chicken. All three hens in my collection have laid and two have incubated, but the eggs have never been fertile. I think pairing has not taken place, the cocks never troubling to do more than feed their partners and more usually neglecting them entirely!

if tame, are also exceedingly jealous of one another.

With other birds these cockatoos are very inoffensive and if they do make a hostile demonstration it is as much from nervousness as real anger. A cock Crimson-winged Parakeet I once kept with some Banksians

Black Cockatoos usually moult in spring, but the moult is not a very thorough one, only a portion of the feathers being cast each year. A hen Banksian, like a Grey Parrot, may lay within a day or two of dropping some feathers. Tame Banksians can be trained to fly at liberty, but they need

constant watching and shepherding for several days until they have learned their way about, discovered their feeding place and overcome their fear of flying down from a height. Untamed birds are a very risky proposition and if turned out at all really need to be first released with cut wings.

Banksians are rather sensitive to tuberculosis. Many years ago the writer foolishly placed a very old and decrepit Roseate Cockatoo in the Banksians' aviary. After a time it fell ill and died, and proved to be badly infected with the disease. A little while later three Barksians went wrong, and one died and also proved to be tubercular. The others I fully expected to lose as well, for they went as thin as rails. However, I caged them in a very warm room and fed them on rich

The Salmon-crested Cockatoo is white, tinged with salmon pink. Its crest is long, broad and salmon colored.

food with quantities of oak-apple grubs. The older hen seemed in great pain. She constantly vomited, became very cross and irritable and continually tore up large quantities of rotten wood with which I provided her. Gradually, however, the symptoms abated and to my intense astonishment both she and her companion began to improve and eventually made a complete recovery. The old hen is still alive twelve years after her illness and recently laid eggs. The younger hen also lived some time and had grown into a magnificent bird when she was lost by an accident.

The mysterious-looking Funereal Cockatoo.

Female Banksians are harder to tame than males and are less good-tempered when their fear is overcome. But, while they threaten and snap when there are cage bars or aviary wire between them and their visitor, they seldom do much if he goes inside with them. When I was able to keep her at liberty, I often carried my old hen "Timmie" on my shoulder, and though I had anxious forebodings that she might take a piece out of my cheek or ear, I am thankful to say that she never abused my confidence.

Banksians are not talkers. I have only heard of one, who said "Cocky" in a very small voice quite out of proportion to his size.

As already indicated Banksian Cockatoos are not absolutely hardy and need a little artificial heat during periods of snow or cold fog when they should not be allowed in the open.

Funereal Cockatoo
Zanda funerea
Distribution: South Queensland, New South Wales, Victoria, Tasmania, South Australia.
Adult male: General colour above blackish brown with smoke-brown edges to the feathers of the neck, back, and wings. Crown blackish brown; under surface dark brown with pale yellowish tips to the feathers. A lemon yellow patch in the region of the ear. The lateral tail feathers have a large patch of yellow freckled with brown. Bill whitish. Length twenty-four and three-quarter inches.
Adult female: Said to resemble the male but to be smaller and to have the yellow edgings to the feathers more pronounced.
Immature: Said to resemble the female in having the yellow edgings to the feathers very pronounced.

The Funereal Cockatoo is common in a wild state but extremely rare in confinement, where it appears to be more delicate than the Banksian. I have a photograph of a tame bird which belonged to a resident in Tasmania and was said to be a great pet and much beloved by its owner. A pinioned female in my own possession only survived a few months. She was subject to severe attacks of vomiting, one of which ultimately proved fatal. Rightly or wrongly I attributed her malady to the bad and musty quality of the seed (she was imported during World War I.) Had we been giving her the wrong

98

diet altogether she would presumably have got worse and worse as long as the same seed mixture was continued, but in point of fact she would recover and live for weeks in perfect health on hemp, sunflower, and peanuts before getting another attack. In disposition she was snappy and unfriendly.

In a wild state the Funereal Cockatoo lives largely on the grubs of woodboring beetles, as well as on seeds. It is said to have a harsh, grating cry sounding like a guttural "Keow."

Gang-gang Cockatoo
Callocorydon fimbriatus
Distribution: New South Wales, Victoria, Tasmania.
Adult male: General colour dusky slate with lighter margins to the feathers. Some of the feathers on the lower abdomen barred with white and orange-red. Flights and tail dark grey. Head scarlet with short erectile crest of soft, loose, curly feathers. Bill horn-grey. Length fourteen and one-eighth inches. Size about that of a pigeon.
Adult female: Upper surface more boldly marked than in the male. Breast and abdomen barred with dull orange and greenish white. Head grey.
Immature: The cock in first plumage has only the red crest and a few small red feathers on the head.

The Gang-gang Cockatoo will sometimes live in a cage, becoming fond of its owner and sometimes learning to say a few words, but most caged birds become feather-pluckers and it is too noisy to be a pleasant companion in a room. As an aviary bird it is one of the most desirable of the cockatoos, for, though it is less beautifully coloured than the Leadbeater and

Salmon-crest, it is irresistibly quaint and amusing. The red-headed cock and his grey mate are the most comical Darby and Joan imaginable, with their chubby faces and quizzical brown eyes. They are much attached to each other and indulge in a continual flow of small talk in a

A pair of Gang-gang Cockatoos, the male quite conspicuous with its scarlet head.

minor key, which occasionally develops into a duet of a more audible and by no means harmonious description. When on the wing they continually utter a loud screeching "Ky-or-ark!" Their flight bears a very close resemblance to that of the Short-eared Owl. They have the same long, round tipped wings, the

Cockatoos and Cockatiel

The Slender-billed Cockatoo is white, tinged with sulphur yellow, and its throat is pink. Noted for its long and slender bill.

same method of alighting and the same complete noiselessness. When acclimatized they are indifferent to cold and will breed readily in a suitable aviary.

Both sexes incubate, the cock sitting on the eggs quite as much as his partner. When rearing young, they should be supplied with whole wheat, rye, or other dark bread moistened with milk.

Toward other cockatoos the Gang-gang is rather savage and aggressive, particularly when kept in pairs.

The food should consist of a seed mixture of one part canary, two parts sunflower, and one part oats. Unlike most cockatoos, they are fond of apple. A fresh turf is also appreciated. The species is very prone to feather plucking and a constant supply of branches *must* be kept in the aviary for the birds to bite up the entire day.

The Gang-gang Cockatoo does well at liberty, and a pair will often stay and nest in the vicinity of their owner's home if care be taken to allow the cock to be loose for several months before his mate is allowed to join him. If an additional precaution is desired, male and female can be let out alternately, each for some months at a time, before they are allowed their freedom together. Gang-gangs range to some distance from their feeding place and they are exceedingly fond of the seeds of thuja and cypress, and are apt to subject these trees to a rather severe pruning in the process of obtaining their favourite delicacy. Consequently, it is inadvisable to keep this species at liberty when you have near neighbours who are particular about their ornamental evergreens, or, it may be added, about their apples and walnuts.

A pair at my old home nested in an oak tree in the garden, but as the cock had only one leg the eggs were infertile. It may be observed that a male parrot, unlike a male finch, is always useless for breeding if his leg or foot be severely damaged. Even a hen so mutilated is of little value.

White-tailed Black Cockatoo
Zanda baudini
Distribution: Southwestern Australia.
Adult: Brownish black, feathers tipped with pale buff. A whitish patch in the region of the ear. An incomplete white bar across the tail. Bill lead colour. Length twenty-three inches.

Young birds of this species were imported by Mr. Frostick many years ago, and fed by hand on sponge cake and hard-boiled egg. He had difficulty in inducing them to take to seed and they unfortunately succumbed to fits, no doubt by reason of the too-stimulating properties of the egg. He describes them as charmingly tame and intelligent, but even at an early age tremendous wood-biters. Possibly, sterner measures would have forced the birds to adopt a more wholesome diet. The Black Cockatoos have tremendous powers of fasting and a hunger-strike of a few days does them no harm whatever.

Roseate Cockatoo
Eolophus roseicapillus
Distribution: Widely distributed over the interior of the Australian Continent.

Adult male: Back, wings, and tail hoary grey, paler on the lower back, rump, and upper tail-coverts. Flight feathers darker grey; crown of head and hind neck pinkish white; throat, sides of face, breast, abdomen, and under wing-coverts rich rose-pink, deepening considerably, without a moult, at the approach of the breeding season. Feet and legs mealy black. Bill greyish white. Iris so dark in colour as to appear black. Length fourteen and three-quarter inches. Size roughly that of a wood-pigeon. Both sexes have a short erectile crest.

Adult female: Similar to the male but slightly more slender in build. Iris hazel or reddish, providing an easy indication of sex.

Immature: In first plumage have the pink of the breast paler and considerably tinged with grey. Adult plumage is assumed with the first complete moult which in English-bred birds begins in the spring following the year of their birth. I am inclined to think that the sexual distinction in the colour of the eye is slight or absent in birds under a year old.

The Roseate Cockatoo is exceedingly abundant in its native land and is also the best known member of its genus in Europe, hundreds being imported annually and sold at a low price—some being offered (usually at a higher price!) as "Australian Grey Parrots."

Many writers have described the beauty of a large flock of "Galahs" in a wild state. "Usually when the weather is broken and unsettled, though, often on a windy winter morning, or in

The Roseate Cockatoo is rose-pink with pinkish white crown.

thundery weather in March or April, against the grey masses of cloud which bank up, forming a sombre background, it would seem as if all the Galahs in the vicinity had gathered in one flock, shrieking and screaming as they circle high in the air, all beating their wings in perfect unison. So, as it were at a given signal, the delicate rose-coloured breasts are all turned the one way, making a beautiful glow of colour as the birds veer 'round; then, with one beat the flock seems almost to have disappeared, just a glimpse of silvery grey flashing as they turn their backs; then a mere speck where each bird is flying, so small that one would hardly believe it to be a bird, so almost invisible does the grey become; then a flash of silvery light before the glow of their breasts flashes into view again."

From the avicultural point of view the Roseate Cockatoo possesses a good many virtues and some failings. As a talker it has seldom much merit, though a hand-reared bird may learn to say a few words. Like nearly all

In their native Australia, Roseate Cockatoos are considered destructive by farmers and are shot or poisoned.

cockatoos, it can, when excited, yell distractingly and if kept in an aviary no unprotected woodwork will long survive the attacks of its beak. On the other hand, it is easily tamed and becomes devotedly attached to its owner, females being often so gentle as to allow even strangers to handle them with impunity. It is intelligent and playful, and, although one cannot help feeling some regret at keeping in close confinement a bird which takes such an evident joy in flight, it will take quite kindly to cage life.

The Roseate Cockatoo should be fed on a seed mixture consisting of two parts canary, one part hemp, one part oats, one part sunflower, and one part peanuts. Raw carrot or any kind of wholesome green food may be offered and a fresh turf of grass is usually much appreciated. Fruit may be given, but is seldom much relished. A small log of wood, preferably with the bark on, will provide the bird with much amusement and exercise for its beak. On no account should a Roseate Cockatoo or any other parrot of similar size be kept in so small a cage that it has not room to flap its extended wings. How many unhappy birds are immured for life in miserable little bell-shaped cages where they have hardly room to turn around! Would that I could confine their owners in similar prisons! Pet Roseates can often be allowed greater liberty if the flight feathers of one wing are kept cut. They love walking about a lawn, eating roots and digging in the turf and will even breed thus under favourable conditions. Many years ago I successfully reared two young from a cut-winged pair that had the run of a grass quadrangle in the centre of the house.

Cockatoos and Cockatiel

Roseates love a rain bath and should have regular opportunities for indulging in it. In warm weather they may be stood out in a shower or in winter sprayed with tepid water. If a cockatoo or parrot feels the need of a bath it will ruffle its feathers and spread its wings as the drops begin to fall on it, and the bath may be safely continued as long as the bird shows its desire for further wetting; when it seems to have had enough it should be put in a fairly warm place until dry. If, however, the bird shows from the first a persistent desire to escape from the moisture, the bath should not be forced upon it or a chill may result. Parrots are generally very wise in the matter of their ablutions, seldom bathing to their own hurt, or refusing a bath when their health and plumage need it.

Few people are willing to provide so common a bird as the Rose-breasted Cockatoo with aviary accommodation, especially as the need for covering every bit of woodwork with strong one-half inch mesh wire netting makes the initial cost of the aviary rather high. On the other hand, there are few foreign birds which nest more readily with suitable encouragement. In a twenty-four foot by eight foot aviary I have bred Roseates without the least trouble. They lose no time about settling down and a rough-plumaged wild hen imported in mid-winter will be rearing young the following July. They are not particular about their nesting site, using either a barrel or a natural tree trunk. In a wild state the birds are said to lay four or five eggs and to line their nest with green leaves. In captivity two or three eggs are the usual clutch. The hen does most of the sitting but her mate relieves her when

Goffin's Cockatoo is native to the Tanimbar Islands and grows to a length of 11½ inches.

she comes off to feed. Incubation lasts about four weeks and the young are a considerable time in the nest. When first hatched they are naked and hideous little objects. Their parents feed them on regurgitated food, holding their beaks and administering the nourishment with a rapid jerking motion quite different from the action of a feeding parakeet. When hungry the babies keep up a hoarse grumbling whine which changes to a rapid "Ek-ek-ek-ek-ek" as soon as they are dependent on their father and mother for some weeks after leaving the nest. Roseate Cockatoos have an amusing habit of correcting their offspring with a peck should they keep on nagging for food without reasonable excuse. Very few birds discipline their brood in this way; either they submit to any amount of badgering without retaliation, or else they get completely tired of them and send them packing for good and all. Dark bread soaked in milk should be provided for birds with young.

A male and female Roseate are a very devoted couple throughout the year and even when the breeding season is over it is a pretty sight to see the hen walk up to her mate, lean across his breast and gently preen the further side of his neck while he lovingly fondles that part of her person which happens to be within most convenient reach. Faithful as they are to one another during life the partners are not, however, unreasonably slow in consoling themselves should death remove male or

The White-crested Cockatoo is noted for its long, broad, white crest.

female. The survivor, on being introduced to a new mate, will make a few conversational remarks, sidle up fairly close and start to preen his feathers. The stranger will do the same. At intervals, as the toilet proceeds they drift a step or two nearer until finally, when they are almost touching, one or other will cautiously nibble the head beside him and if the salute is well received the simple courtship is ended. Few foreign birds present a more charming spectacle at liberty than a pair of Roseate Cockatoos. Their flight, though not particularly rapid, is very buoyant and when in a playful mood, as they often are, they indulge in a most fascinating display of aerial gymnastics, swooping and twisting and shrieking with excitement and *joie de vivre*. The adults also possess the recommendation of being too big for owls to tackle; absolutely indifferent to cold; and practically harmless to growing fruit. Unfortunately, however, the Roseate Cockatoo has certain failings as a liberty bird which somewhat discount its good points. Pairs are decidedly difficult to induce to stay, while at the best of times they range far from home so that it is necessary to warn neighbours in order that they may not be accidentally shot. Hens, if left at liberty throughout the year, usually try to breed in cold weather and succumb to egg-laying troubles.

Lastly, young birds are delicate during the first twelve months of their lives. If bred at liberty they often die shortly after leaving the nest and in any case they are unable to survive the first winter without artificial heat. To get the best results it is desirable to obtain an adult pair and turn them into a movable aviary. It should be possible to shut the birds into the shelter so that later the young may get the benefit of the warmth of a portable heating apparatus during the cold season. If all goes well, the first autumn should see you with a couple of youngsters of your own breeding. As soon as these are able to feed themselves the old cock can be turned loose. He will never stray so long as his mate is confined, but should she die or fall ill and have to be taken indoors, he should be caught up at once or you may lose him. The young birds can be left with their mother until the cock is put back in April, unless she begins to show signs of being spiteful with them sooner, in which case they must be removed immediately. In favourable climates one youngster can be given his liberty at the end of May, but in places where birds thrive indifferently it is better to wait until he has completed his first moult. The second young bird should not be let out before the old cock is again released at the close of the second breeding season. If the first year's young survive the winter and prove a true pair the owner can please himself whether he will let them breed at liberty their third summer or catch them up in order to make sure of the brood surviving. In any case, it will be unwise to allow the hen to winter out, once she has become mature, for the reason already given. Cock Roseates, whose mates are confined, have an annoying habit of destroying the woodwork of aviaries in close proximity to their wives' abodes. For this reason it is necessary to place the hens' aviaries not less than fifty yards from any vulnerable woodwork and to make sure that they are completely wired outside as well as inside.

Tame Roseate Cockatoos when kept at liberty sometimes develop an odd fondness for mechanical travel. A hen bird, the property of a butcher on Hayling Island, was for some years quite

The Funereal Cockatoo, also known as the Black Cockatoo.

a well-known figure by reason of her fondness for riding on motor cars. She would settle on the back of a car and, after enjoying a spin of a mile or two, would fly back to her home. Another hen which I gave to a gentleman in France repaired to the local railway station and spent her time

Mutual preening is part of the courtship of Sulphur-crested Cockatoos.

riding on the engines until her plumage was blackened with smoke!

Hybrids have been produced between the Roseate Cockatoo and the Greater and Lesser Sulphur-crests.

Far more amazing is the production of fertile eggs as the result of a mating between a hen Roseate and a cock Rosella Parakeet. Unfortunately the Cockatoo sat unsteadily (no doubt expecting the Rosella to take his turn on the eggs after the manner of gentlemen of her own race), and she fell ill and died before the period of incubation was completed. Had young been reared it would indeed have been interesting to see how nature solved the puzzle of fusing two birds so totally different in form, voice and, most of all, colour!

In mixed company the Roseate is a fairly peaceful bird when not breeding, but it becomes decidedly aggressive when it has young to defend.

A very pretty variety is occasionally seen in which the grey areas of the normal plumage are replaced by white, the pink being retained. A pair of these albinistic birds are at present living in my collection.

Greater Sulphur-crested Cockatoo
Kakatoe galerita
Distribution: Widely distributed over Australia.
Adult male: White, with sulphur yellow crest, under surface of tail and inner webs of primary and secondary quills. Bill black. Iris almost black. Total length twenty inches.
Adult female: Resembles the male, but is said to have a slightly paler iris, though this is doubtful.
Immature: Said to resemble the adults.

The Sulphur-crested Cockatoo is a very common bird in Australia, congregating in large flocks and laying its two white eggs, either in hollow trees or in holes excavated in the face of a cliff. One observer writes, "They are found all year along the (Murray) river and a great distance back. They congregate in great numbers at nesting time and take possession of the holes worn by the weather into the high cliffs rising several hundreds of feet out of the water; here they lay their eggs upon the bare sand and hatch out their young. It is a very interesting sight to see many hundreds of these birds half out of their nesting holes or sitting upon the ledges of rock near their nests; depressing and raising their beautiful yellow crests. They are very noisy birds and keep up a continual screeching call."

The Sulphur-crested Cockatoo is very destructive to growing crops and is much hated by the farmers, who kill them wholesale either by scattering poisoned grain, or by putting poison into drinking places. While appreciating the point of view of the settlers whose livelihood is threatened, this terribly cruel method of destruction is much to be regretted, as not only are the chief offenders killed, but numbers of rare, beautiful, and sometimes harmless birds perish with them. It is particularly hard that the Australian authorities should place every obstacle in the way of the export of so many kinds of birds, even under humane conditions and for the purposes of legitimate aviculture, when every year thousands are poisoned and the bodies left to rot on the ground.

As a cage bird the Sulphur-crested Cockatoo is hardy and enduring and there are records of individuals living to a stupendous age—over one hundred years in a few cases. The bird becomes very tame and much attached to its owner, sometimes allowing even strangers to handle it with impunity. It also makes a fair talker, but, like all its tribe, is given in moments of excitement to yelling in the most appalling fashion.

The Sulphur-crest is perfectly hardy in an outdoor aviary, though needing the strongest material to resist its powerful beak. When suitably housed it is quite ready to go to nest. I am a little uncertain as to whether the colour of the iris is a reliable guide as to sex in this species. Mr. Whitley, who owns a breeding pair, informs me that his hen has a slightly paler eye than her mate, but I have only once seen a Sulphur-crest with an eye that did not look boot-button black, so if the light iris is always characteristic of the female, the number of hens must be exceedingly small.

In disposition the Sulphur-crest is inclined to be somewhat aggressive to other parrot-like birds of large size.

The Palm Cockatoo is the largest of all parrot species.

At liberty this species has been kept with some measure of success and young have been reared. Although a handsome and imposing bird on the wing it is decidedly destructive to trees and is inclined to range some distance from home. Cock and hen should be released alternately for some months before they are allowed free together.

At Lilford, hybrids between this species and the Roseate Cockatoo were produced at liberty.

*The Blue-eyed Cockatoo (*Kakatoe ophthalmica*).*

The Sulphur-crested Cockatoo should be given a seed mixture of one part canary, one part oats, one part hemp, one part sunflower, and one part peanuts, with any raw vegetables it will eat, except potatoes. Fruit may be offered, though it is seldom greatly relished. Tea, coffee, meat, and butter should never be given. This cockatoo must have made its first appearance in England a surprisingly long time ago, as a portrait by Simon Verelot, painted about the middle of the seventeenth century,

shows a little girl with a pet bird unmistakably belonging to this species.

Blue-eyed Cockatoo
Kakatoe ophthalmica
Distribution: New Britain.
Adult: White. Part of crest lemon yellow. A faint yellow tinge on the inner webs of some of the flights and tail feathers. Naked skin 'round eyes blue. Bill black. Total length nineteen inches.

A rarely imported bird. Its disposition and needs are the same as the Sulphur-crest's.

Lesser Sulphur-crested Cockatoo
Kakatoe sulphurea
Distribution: Celebes, Buton and Togian Islands.
Adult male: White with a faint yellow tinge on the breast and a more pronounced one on the under surface of the quills and tail. Crest long, pointed and lemon yellow. A yellow patch on the cheeks. Iris practically black. Bill black. Length thirteen inches.
Adult female: Has a red iris.

The Lesser Sulphur-crest does not do very well in a cage, but is hardy and enduring in an outdoor aviary, or at liberty. It is very noisy and seldom a good talker, but, like all white cockatoos, is easily tamed. The food should be that of the Greater Sulphur-crest: green peas and green wheat are much appreciated.

Both sexes sit, the cock quite as much as, if not more than, the hen. The period of incubation is twenty-four days. The species has been bred in captivity and hybrids with the Roseate have also been reared.

Leadbeater's Cockatoo
Loppochroa leadbeateri
Distribution: New South Wales, Victoria, South Australia,

Southwest and Northwest Australia.

Adult male: Back, wings, and tail white. Inner webs of primary and secondary quills and inner tail-feathers red. Sides of face, hind-neck, chin, breast, sides of body, and under wing-coverts salmon-pink. Base of forehead dull rose-red. The long crest is red at the base, then yellow, then red, and then white. Bill whitish. Iris practically black. Total length fifteen inches.

Adult female: Resembles the male, but has the iris hazel or reddish.

Immature: Said to resemble the adult.

An observer writing of this very lovely cockatoo in a wild state says, "As far as I know only the flamingo exhibits such a beautiful rosy flush, contrasting with snowy white. The birds seem quite aware of their beauty and spend much of their time showing off to one another. By opening their wings partially, they exhibit the pink colour underneath, at the same time spreading the magnificent crest with its bands of yellow and scarlet until it forms a perfect semi-circle. If I had not seen it done repeatedly I could not have believed that the crest could be spread so far forward, the front a layer of pebbles four or five inches deep in the nests of these birds, immediately below the debris of leaves and wood in which the two eggs lay.

Leadbeater's Cockatoo will live quite well in a cage, but although tame individuals which say a word or two are by no means rare, it has the reputation of being less easy to demonstrate than its near allies. Its voice is exceedingly unpleasant, a loud, quavering scream uttered in a harassed tone, and when frightened or angry it emits a truly hideous din.

Leadbeater's Cockatoo is also known as Major Mitchell's Cockatoo.

As an aviary bird it is exceedingly hardy and a free breeder. I knew a pair which lived for many years in a small ramshackle fowl run in Scotland. They nested each season and on the first occasion nearly reared their young which were killed by rats when almost ready to fly. In subsequent years the chicks were weakly and did not survive long, doubtless owing to the parents' loss of stamina through cramped quarters and lack of fresh ground.

Both sexes incubate the eggs, the male sitting quite as much as, and indeed more than, his mate. The young when being fed make a noise like young Roseates.

The species is spiteful in mixed company.

Leadbeater's Cockatoo has been kept and bred at liberty and

Because of its powerful and destructive beak, the Salmon-crested Cockatoo's need to gnaw should be satisfied by branches of wood.

its management should be the same as that of the Sulphur-crest. Where natural hollow tree-trunks are not available barrels should be put up for the birds to occupy.

A bird of this species has been known to live wild throughout a whole winter in the comparatively wet and bleak climate of Galloway in Scotland.

Citron-crested Cockatoo
Kakatoe citrino-cristata
Distribution: Sumba.
Adult male: White; a long, pointed orange crest. A yellowish patch on the cheek. Under-surface of quills and tail tinged with pale yellow. Bill black. Iris practically black. Total length fourteen inches.
Adult female: Differs from the male in having a red iris.

The Citron-crested Cockatoo is imported at somewhat infrequent intervals. It does not differ from its allies either in disposition or requirements. The food should be

that of the Sulphur-crest. It does better in an aviary than a cage.

Rose or Salmon-crested Cockatoo
Kakatoe moluccensis
Distribution: Ceram and Amboyna.
Adult male: White tinged with salmon-pink, especially on the breast. A long, broad crest with some of the central feathers hairy and deep salmon colour. Under-surface of quills and tail suffused with a yellowish salmon tint. Bill black. Iris practically black. Total length twenty inches.
Adult female: Very similar.

The Salmon-crest is one of the most beautifully coloured of the cockatoos. It has a quaint, solemn appearance and is rather slow in its movements, but it becomes very tame and affectionate and sometimes makes an excellent talker. It is perfectly hardy and can be wintered out-of-doors and it is said to be a good stayer at liberty, though probably destructive to trees. It has nested in a California aviary, but the eggs were destroyed by an accident.

The Salmon-crest's failings consist of a terrific voice, a very powerful and destructive beak, and a rather spiteful disposition towards other birds. It will live quite well in a cage if the cage is very large and plenty of wood is provided for the bird's amusement. The food should consist of a mixture of canary, wheat, oats, and sunflower. Fruit and raw vegetables should be offered.

White-crested Cockatoo
Kakatoe alba
Distribution: Halmahera group of islands.
Adult: White. Crest long and broad. Inner surface of inner webs of flights and tail tinged with pale yellow. Bill black. Length eighteen inches.

The White-crested Cockatoo is in every respect an exact counterpart of its near relative the Salmon-crested. Its virtues and vices are identical and it requires the same treatment and the same precautions to prevent feather-plucking. It has produced hybrids with the Leadbeater when kept at liberty in Norfolk.

Slender-billed Cockatoo
Licmetis teniurostris
Distribution: North and Southwest Australia, South Australia, Victoria, New South Wales.
Adult male: General colour white, tinged with sulphur yellow, especially on the under surface of the tail. Base of feathers on head, throat, neck, and all 'round the breast pink. Base of forehead and a large patch in front of the eye red. Bill whitish horn and upper mandible very long and slender. Eyes dark. Total length seventeen and seven-eighths inches.
Adult female: Said to resemble the male.
Immature: Said to resemble the adults.

An observer, writing of this bird, says: "*Licmetis nasica* lives almost exclusively on a small yam which it digs up with its long bill. Of course, such a vast amount of digging must wear the upper mandible very rapidly, but this is compensated for by the rapidity of its growth. An old pet bird tried to lever a brick out of a drain with its bill and split the upper portion from near the point to the base. I mended the break and in three weeks the split portion had grown down to the point and before the end of the following week no trace of the injury was visible."

The Slender-billed Cockatoo compensates for its somewhat grotesque appearance and

White-crested Cockatoos can be extremely aggressive during the breeding season.

unmusical voice by an absurd amiability when tamed and a fair capacity for learning to talk. It should be fed on a seed mixture of canary, millet, and oats with as many peanuts as it likes to eat, and any raw vegetables that it cares for with the exception of potato and parsley. A good-sized turf should be kept in the cage to provide the bird with amusement and exercise for its digging propensities. The Slender-billed Cockatoo is perfectly hardy in an

In nature, the Slender-billed Corella nests in eucalyptus trees.

aviary and would probably breed if given the encouragement to do so. The sexes appear hard to distinguish and as I have never seen a bird with a light iris, I conclude that the Slender-bill is one of those cockatoos in which the colour of the eye is of no assistance in telling the male from the female.

A pair of these birds I released without special precautions only stayed for a few weeks, but it is possible that they would have become more attached to their home had I first let out male and female, alternately, for some months.

The Western race of the Slender-bill, sometimes known as the Dampier Cockatoo (*Licmetis pastinator*), has been exhibited at the Palace.

Bloodstained Cockatoo
Ducorpsius sanguineus
Distribution: Australia.
Adult male: White; bases of the feathers of head and neck, pink. Some pink in front of and below the eye. Crest short. Inner webs of flights and under surface of tail pale yellow. Bill bluish white. Length sixteen and nine-tenths inches.
Adult female: Smaller than the male.

The Bloodstained Cockatoo, unlike some of its near relatives, appears to be in part, at any rate, a beneficial bird in a wild state, living on the fruit of a creeping, noxious plant called Double-gees whose seeds seriously lame sheep. Certain districts passed laws protecting the birds, but a wise-acre visiting the district (whose opinions we trust were not heeded) pointed out that the protection was a mistake because whole seeds would probably be voided by the Cockatoos and the range of the plant extended. Anybody possessing the most elementary knowledge of a parrot's feeding habits and digestive system would know that the chances of an undigested seed passing through the bird's body are practically nil. Moreover, one would have thought that the thousands of seeds actually assimilated by the cockatoos would, if they had not been eaten, have been a far more likely means of spreading the plant than the one or two supposed to escape destruction! Among birds it is not *seed* eaters which are seed distributors, but *berry* eaters.

Three eggs are usually laid, and the nest is situated in a hollow in a tree, cliff-face, or large termite mound. In captivity the Bloodstained Cockatoo makes a docile and affectionate pet and a good talker. It can be wintered out-of-doors, but, like all its family, it is addicted to screaming.

It should be fed like the Gang-gang Cockatoo. Hemp is absolute poison to it and must never be given. Before the writer discovered this fact he killed two remarkably fine birds in a very short space of time, simply by the free use of hemp and sunflower.

Two birds which I released stayed well, but were so fearfully destructive to trees that I had to get rid of them. They were spiteful with other parrots and with their own species.

Wild birds have been known to evict sitting Roseate Cockatoos, add their own eggs to the clutch, and hatch and rear a mixed brood.

Bare-eyed Cockatoo
Ducorpsius gymnopis

Distribution: South Australia.
Adult male: White. Bases of feathers of head and neck and feathers below and in front of eye, pink. Inner webs of flights and under surface of tail pale yellow. Bill bluish white. Length seventeen inches.
Adult female: Similar but smaller.

The Bare-eyed Cockatoo is in every respect an exact counterpart of the Bloodstained, from which it differs in having a large area of naked blue skin below the eye, whereas the blue skin round the Bloodstained Cockatoo's eye is of equal width above and below. In captivity it makes an exceptionally good-

In the six subspecies of the Lesser Sulphur-crested Cockatoo the crest ranges from light yellow to a deep orange.

tempered, playful and amusing pet, with, however, the family weakness for screaming. It does best when not permanently confined in a parrot cage.

It should be fed on canary, oats, sunflower, and peanuts with any fruit, green food, and raw vegetables that it will eat. Hemp is extremely injurious and causes liver disease in a remarkably short space of time unless the bird has complete freedom.

The Bare-eyed Cockatoo has been bred at the Zoological Gardens in England, and also by an aviculturist in Holland. The young birds remain nine weeks in the nest. Unlike some cockatoos, the sexes of this species do not differ in the colour of the iris, the eyes of both male and female being almost black.

The Bare-eyed Cockatoo is spiteful in mixed company. It can be wintered out-of-doors and will stay at liberty, but is terribly destructive to trees.

Cockatoos and Cockatiel

Cockatiel
Leptolophus hollandicus

Distribution: Widely distributed over the interior of the Australian Continent.

Adult male: General colour above and below dusky brown, more greyish brown on the under surface and blackish on the shoulders and under wing-coverts. Hind neck, mantle, and upper back, smoke brown. Large whitish patch on the wing. Forepart of head, sides of face, throat, and crest lemon yellow, the tips of the crest feathers becoming brown. Ear-coverts bright orange; sides of crown white. Tail fairly long and blackish brown, central feathers projecting beyond the rest. Bill dark horn, eyes brown. Total length thirteen and one-eighth inches. Size roughly that of a thrush, but tail much longer.

Adult female: Bears considerable resemblance to the male, but her wing patch is smaller and of less pure a white, her thighs are barred with pale yellow, her tail is freckled and barred with dark grey and the outer feathers are yellowish. Orange cheek patch present, but lemon and white areas practically absent from the head.

Immature: Much resemble the female, but young males are said to be distinguishable from the time of leaving the nest by a perceptible shade of yellow on the head and face.

Although one of the most soberly coloured members of the parrot family, the Cockatiel has long been popular among aviculturists by reason of its hardiness, prolificacy, and gentle disposition. As pets hens have not much to recommend them, but a hand-reared male will often learn to talk and whistle a little and become much attached to his owner. He is not exactly a silent bird, but there are many worse noises than his shrill "Curryou! Creeou!" If kept in a cage he should always, when sufficiently tamed, be allowed to take daily flying exercise in a room.

The Cockatiel should be fed on canary, millet, hemp, and oats, together with green food.

As aviary birds Cockatiels have much to recommend them. Healthy, unrelated pairs are very free breeders, often rearing two or three broods of six or seven. If permitted to do so, they will go on nesting far into the winter, but in the English climate it is very desirable to restrict breeding to the warmer months of the year, so the nest logs should be

A pair of Cockatiels; the male has more yellow on its head.

removed in October and not put back before April is well advanced. It is not wise to keep more than one pair of Cockatiels in the same aviary while breeding is going on, as they squabble a good bit among themselves. With other species of birds they are usually safe, but their restless habits are sometimes disturbing to the peace of mind of small finches.

As with some of the cockatoos, the male Cockatiel assists his mate in the duties of incubation. No nesting material is needed, a little earth or moist decayed wood being all that the eggs require to rest on. The log should be roomy, as the Cockatiel has no fondness for cramped quarters.

Unfortunately, while healthy Cockatiels are hardy and prolific, there are often on the market a number of birds inbred or badly reared that are a source of trouble to their purchasers, the cocks proving sterile and the hens getting egg-bound or indulging in some physical or mental vagaries that effectually prevent the propagation of their kind. It is to be hoped that some day breeders of foreign birds will begin to observe the elementary rules of hygiene and management that no one engaged in rearing domestic animals would think of neglecting.

As a liberty bird the Cockatiel is one of the most unpromising subjects I have tried. A migrant and wanderer in his own land, his attachment to his home is remarkably small. The only way to enjoy his very beautiful and extremely powerful flight is to train one cock of a breeding pair as a day-liberty bird. The hen's aviary must be placed in a conspicuous position near tall trees with the roosting and feeding aviary alongside. The

cock's first release should take place on a calm winter morning when the trees are bare, as a Cockatiel has a rooted objection to settling on any branch that has leaves on it. He should also be turned out before he has had his breakfast and his general training and management should be the same as that of a Barraband—not forgetting the danger of allowing him to be loose in a snowstorm. As long as he is the only one of his kind at liberty and his wife remains in the aviary as a decoy he may stay and behave himself, but allow him even one

The Cockatiel can be taught to speak a few words and whistle short tunes.

companion in freedom—and that a male—and the chances are you will see him no more.

Some years ago I had a cut-winged pair of Cockatiels which nested in the grass quadrangle where Roseate Cockatoos reared young. Unfortunately the hen was taken by an owl and the cock soon afterwards deserted the eggs.

In Australia the Cockatiel is sometimes known as "Cockatoo-parrot" and "Quarrion."

Macaws

Red and Yellow Macaw
Ara macao
Distribution: Mexico and Central America.
Adult: Scarlet; feathers of the central part of the wing showing a mixture of red, green, and yellow. Flights and lower edge of the wing blue. Rump pale blue. Some greenish blue and olive feathers at the sides of the rump and on the thighs. Central tail feathers of great length; scarlet with a purplish blue tinge at the base and tips. Outer tail feathers blue; some reddish chocolate near the base. Upper mandible whitish. Length thirty-six inches.
Immature: Greener on the wings.

The large macaws, of which this gigantic and gaudy bird is a typical example, are easily tamed and have a fair capacity for learning to talk. They are perfectly hardy, can be wintered out-of-doors, and they are usually fairly safe in mixed company. Among their chief failings are voices in proportion to their size and beaks which only the strongest aviary can resist. It is customary to keep them chained by one leg to a perch, but this is not fair or humane treatment for creatures that are active, playful, and intelligent. There are really only three tolerable ways of keeping macaws—in aviaries, at complete liberty, and with cut wings in enclosures from which they cannot escape by climbing.

The Red and Yellow Macaw is usually gentle with a person to whom he is attached, but it is extremely risky to make advances to a strange macaw unless he be of one of the all-blue species. It is recorded that an untamed and savage Red and Yellow actually killed a bull terrier after a Homeric combat in which both its wings were broken.

Undoubtedly the Red and Yellow Macaw shows to best advantage as a liberty bird. In a state of freedom it is said to be far less noisy and destructive than might be expected and tame single birds, or pairs—one member of which is tame—are reputed not to leave the neighbourhood of their homes.

Macaws should be fed on a mixture one-half of which consists of peanuts, while canary, hemp, sunflower, oats, and wheat make up the remainder. Plenty of fruit is a necessity. Very young birds benefit by a diet of bread and milk or milk pudding.

The female Red and Yellow Macaw have been bred. A very large barrel partly filled with decayed wood, or a hollow tree trunk, makes the best nest.

Red and Blue Macaw
Ara chloroptera
Distribution: Guatemala to Guiana.
Adult: Crimson. Mantle crimson

The Red and Yellow Macaw is also known as the Scarlet Macaw.

mixed with olive green. Wings olive green mixed with slate blue. Flights blue. Under wing-coverts red. Rump pale blue. Feathers at the sides of the rump tinged with olive. Central tail feathers dark red with blue tips. Outer tail feathers maroon at the base; blue at the tips. Bill horn -white. Total length thirty-four inches.

A well-known bird, imported as early as the end of the sixteenth century. It is as hardy as other macaws and has the same disposition and needs.

The female is said to be smaller, with a shorter beak. It has hybridized with the Military Macaw.

Blue and Yellow Macaw
Ara ararauna
Distribution: Tropical America from Panama to Guiana.
Adult: Blue, darker on the flights and tail. Sides of neck, entire breast, and under wing-coverts yellow. Throat blackish with an outer edging of greyish olive or greenish feathers. Some black feathers on the naked skin of the cheeks. Bill black. Total length thirty-one inches.

A freely imported and well-known bird which is the best talker of the genus, some specimens being very talented. It usually becomes attached to one person or one sex, being inclined to bite strangers. It is perfectly hardy and a good stayer at liberty, with the possible exception of very shy individuals with equally untamed mates. Like many macaws it is capable of blushing when excited, the bare skin of the face becoming suffused with pink.

Early in the last century a pair of these macaws bred freely in France, laying sixty-two eggs and rearing fifteen young which spent three months in the nest.

The female is said to be smaller, with a shorter and narrower beak.

*Military Macaw (*Ara militaris*).*

Military Macaw
Ara militaris
Distribution: Mexico, Central and South America.
Adult: Olive green, more golden brown on the wings and brighter and bluer on the head. Forehead red. Rump pale blue. Flights and lower edge of the wing blue. Central tail feathers wine red at the base; blue at the tip. Outer tail feathers mainly blue. Bill blackish. Length twenty-seven inches.

Fairly often imported and likely to make a good talker. Treatment as for other large macaws. Hybrids between this species and the Red and Blue have been known.

Lear's Macaws are native to Brazil.

The female is said to be smaller, with a shorter and more arched beak.

Glaucous Macaw
Anodorhyncus glaucus
Distribution: Paraguay, Uruguay, and Southern Brazil.
Adult: Slate blue, brighter on the rump and very dull on the head, neck and upper breast. A patch of naked yellow skin on the cheek. Bill thick. Total length twenty-nine inches.

A rarely imported bird resembling other large all-blue macaws in disposition and hardiness.

Lear's Macaw
Anodorhyncus leari
Distribution: Brazil.
Adult: Hyacinth blue. Head and neck paler and more slate coloured. Breast feathers with paler tips. Bill black. A patch of naked yellow skin on the cheek. Length twenty-eight and one-half inches.

Lear's Macaw differs from its close ally, the Hyacinthine, in its slightly smaller size and less richly coloured head and breast. Unmated birds are gentle, friendly creatures and, though they can certainly make themselves heard, they screech somewhat less raucously than their parti-coloured relatives, their voices, as Mr. Astley noted, having something of the carrion crow timbre about them.

The species is excessively hardy. A bird in my possession, when in rough importation plumage, flew into the top of a bare oak tree and stayed there for more than forty-eight hours during a spell of raw January weather. When at length he decided to come down he was not a penny the worse for his long fast and exposure.

Lear's, like Hyacinthines, are bad stayers at liberty. After a lot of trouble I did manage to induce

118

a couple to settle down for some months, but both eventually strayed and were shot. The hen used to gratify her taste for society by flying daily to a town three miles distant where she amused herself by pulling out the pegs of people's clothes lines and playing with the dogs. She was sometimes bitten, but such an embarassing occurrence did not make her any less fond of her canine companions.

Hyacinthine Macaw
Anodorhyncus hyacinthinus
Distribution: Central Brazil.
Adult: Deep hyacinth blue. A patch of bare yellow skin at the base of the beak. Bill black and very large. Total length thirty-four inches.

The Hyacinthine Macaw is certainly one of the most remarkable of living birds. Its great size, immense curved beak, and wonderful garb of uniform: deep, hyacinth blue make it, if not one of the most elegant of its family, at least the most imposing. Single birds are very gentle and affectionate, though, as with other macaws and indeed most parrots, the presence of a female companion will often make a cock Hyacinthine somewhat unfriendly towards humanity. The species is extremely hardy and, provided it escapes the miserable fate of being chained permanently by one leg to a perch, will live for a great number of years, showing itself wholly indifferent to cold in an outdoor aviary. It is unfortunately a bad stayer at liberty, even tame birds going straight off and flying for miles, being usually shot in mistake for a hawk.

The Hyacinthine should be fed like other macaws, and when very young benefits by being given bread and milk. ·

The Hyacinthine Macaw is admired for its deep hyacinth blue coloration.

Severe Macaw
Ara severa
Distribution: Brazil, Amazon Valley, Guiana, Colombia, Panama.
Adult: Dark green, a bluish tinge on the crown and lower edge of the wing. A dark brown band across the forehead and some dark greenish brown feathers on the edge of the cheeks. Outer webs of flights slate-blue. Under wing-coverts mainly red. Tail reddish brown at the base and on the under surface; remainder blue-green. Bill black. Total length twenty inches.

The smaller macaws have the reputation of being intelligent and affectionate pets with some talent for talking and no worse proclivity for screaming than Amazons. They do quite well in cages if let out for daily exercise. As to their

Macaws

A pair of Illiger's Macaws.

the tip. Bill horn black. Total length sixteen and three-quarter inches. Smaller than the Severe Macaw.
Adult female: Said to have less red on the forehead.
Immature: Said to have less red on the forehead and the red patches on the body replaced by yellowish colour; upper parts spotted with pale grey-brown.

Illiger's Macaw is said to make a very affectionate pet and a fair talker. One in Miss Knobel's collection was most playful and amusing and loved emptying the waste paper basket and distributing the contents over the floor. His one failing was a

The Severe Macaw is also known as the Chestnut-fronted Macaw.

ability to stand cold there seems to be little information. They should be fed like Blue-fronted Amazons. A Severe Macaw in Miss Knobel's possession was devoted to his mistress and liked climbing about her and lying in her lap. He talked a good deal, but with indistinct articulation.

Illiger's Macaw
Ara maracana
Distribution: Brazil and Paraguay.
Adult male: Dark green. Forehead red. Crown and cheeks bluish; also lower edge of wing. Flights bluish slate. Some red feathers in the centre of the abdomen and on the upper rump. Tail brown and olive at the base; blue-green at

fondness for nipping his mistress's ankles, a form of practical joking to which many parrots are addicted. He bathed freely and talked in an amusing way.

A pair on the Continent hatched a young one, but did not rear it. The cock fed the hen while she was sitting and the pair were very spiteful to other birds. Like the larger macaws, the small species, when young, should be given bread and milk.

Nomenclature of the feathers of the wing: On this macaw the primary feathers are colored brown, the secondaries grey. The greater coverts of the secondaries are shown in light green, while the lesser and median wing coverts appear in blue.

Suggested Reading

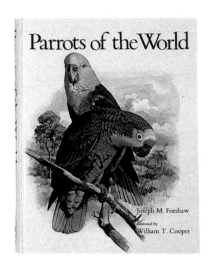

PARROTS OF THE WORLD by Joseph M. Forshaw (PS-753)

Every species and subspecies of parrot in the world, including those recently extinct, is covered in this authoritative work. Almost 500 species or subspecies appear in the color illustrations by William T. Cooper. Descriptions are accompanied by distribution maps and accounts of behavior, feeding habits, and nesting. *Almost 300 color plates. Hard cover, 9½ × 12½", 584 pp.*

make sure that their parrot becomes truly a pet and companion, instead of just an avian boarder in the home, *Training Your Parrot* contains exactly the kind of sensible, practical, experience-proved advice that all parrot owners can put to good use. Written by one pet owner for other pet owners, all the suggestions are based on first-hand experience. Chapters covering selection, housing and equipment, daily care, taming, and speech training are filled with specific instances of the author's experiences with Siegfried, his own amazon parrot, to illustrate the principles of taming and training that apply to all parrots, whatever the species. *Illustrated with 72 color and 57 black-and-white photos and drawings. Hard cover, 5½ × 8", 192 pp.*

TRAINING YOUR PARROT by Kevin Murphy (H-1056)

Addressed to people who want to

PARROTS AND RELATED BIRDS by Henry Bates and Robert Busenbark (H-912)

This is the "bible" for parrot lovers. It has more color photographs and more information on parrot keeping than any other single book on the subject. Chapters on parrots in aviculture, feeding, housing, taming, talking, breeding, and

hand-rearing are followed by sections on the various groups and particular species.
Illustrated with 107 black-and-white and 160 color photos. Hard cover, 5½ × 8½", 543 pp.

DISEASES OF PARROTS by Elisha Burr (H-1037)

In the only book devoted exclusively to the diseases of psittacine birds, Dr. Burr provides an up-to-date coverage of diagnosis and treatment. Introductory material on anatomy and physiology, general care, and nutrition lays the groundwork for chapters on examination and diagnostic procedures, response to accidents and injuries, and control and treatment of diseases associated with the various body systems—respiratory, digestive, urinary, etc. The final chapters address external disorders and problems in breeding and rearing young. Several appendices summarize text discussions and indicate dosages of commonly used medicines.
Illustrated with over 150 color and black-and-white photos. Hard cover, 5½ × 8", 320 pp.

SMALL PARROTS by David Seth-Smith (H-1017)

The complete text of Smith's 1926 classic is reprinted with its origi-

nal full color lithographs, reproduced in their original style. This 1979 edition, revised by Dr. Matthew M. Vriends, has an additional 12 full color photographic plates of popular parrots. Also included is a separate index showing both the common and taxonomic names by which the birds are identified in this volume, and also their currently accepted names. This updated classic is a practical maintenance and breeding guide to cockatiels, conures, lovebirds and more, based on the author's firsthand observations.
Illustrated with 44 color drawings and photos, and 24 line drawings. Hard cover, 5½ × 8½", 302 pp.

PARROT GUIDE by Cyril H. Rogers (PL-2984)

An abundance of fascinating photographs, illustrates the text that will enable the reader to wisely select a healthy parrot as a pet or breeder. Chapters on care, housing and feeding are included with some chapters on teaching your pet parrot to speak. Also covered are breeding, health and exhibition. Fascinating reading for the parrot owner, or the novice about to choose his first parrot.
Illustrated with 110 color and 82 black-and-white photos, 5½ × 8½", 256 pp.

Index

Amazons can be taught to speak complete sentences and to whistle short tunes.

CO-028 S

A COMPLETE INTRODUCTION TO

PARROTS

A male Australian King Parrot.